Acknowledgements

This book has been inspired by personal experiences,
journeys, and conversations with those I have crossed paths
with on my travels and in life.

Friends and family, you guys are my rocks. Your
unconditional support has made my life what it is now –
for that I thank you.

To those of you who encouraged me to focus on my writing,
I am especially grateful.

Contents

Part Two: Explore Food 105

Part Three: Explore Life 134

Part One: Explore the World

Traveller

/ˈtrav(ə)lə/ noun

A person who makes a journey often.

Introduction

195 countries.

7 continents.

0 – 45 days of paid leave from work.

W hat you do (or want to do) with your life is in your hands, subject to your perceived circumstances, restrictions or limitations.

Before reading this book further, I request that you keep an open mind about how you have been prioritising different aspects of your life, such as:

- You
- Health
- Loved ones
- Work
- Finances
- Recreation
- Travel

Whenever you get the chance, ask yourself if you could find a way to reshuffle a few things and prioritise what you really want to do next.

If you have a job, you should be entitled to paid annual leave (unless you live in Brunei or Kiribati). How do you plan to use your annual leave?

With prioritisation, budget-management, a few weeks of eating instant noodles, replacing your three-ply toilet paper with two, efficient decision-making and negotiations with your boss or family, you can hopefully make some time to explore this planet.

Sources: United Nations, 2019; International Labour Organisation, 2019

The Continents

Millions of years ago, the world's seven continents were just one super-continent.

Thanks to plate tectonics and other reasons beyond my brainpower, this super-continent divided into further land masses, such as *Pangea.*

Eventually, *Pangea* divided further to create additional land masses, including *Gondwana Land,* now known as *Africa, South America, Australia, Antarctica* and *India* (although India broke free and moved to the north, creating the *Himalaya* mountain range).

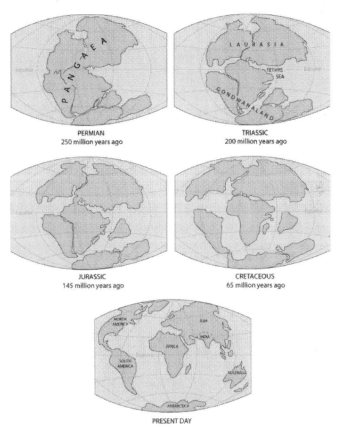

Source: *Livescience.com; Image credit: U.S. Geological Survey*

Asia: Going Back in Time

Asia is one of the largest and most populous continents in the world. With hundreds of languages spoken and multiple religions practised, this continent has some of the most interesting histories to date.

Home to Mount Everest, the highest peak on the planet, Asia hosts some of the most beautiful endangered species on earth, such as the tiger and giant panda.

While travelling through Asia, my observation is that you often feel as if you have stepped back in time.

Whether walking the streets of Samarkand, the presence of their much beloved past King, Emir Timur, can be felt in every step of the journey or when entering the Victoria Memorial in Kolkata, vibes from the British colonial era fill the air and dominate your sensory experience.

Cambodia was particularly interesting; a mostly Buddhist nation co-existing alongside other religions, like Hinduism; a nation also experiencing more recent cruelty at the Killing Fields during the 1970s Khmer regime.

Our Mongol, Greek, Arab, French, Portuguese and, of course, British ancestors have all made attempts to conquer various parts of this rich continent, leaving the locals with both positive and negative aftertastes. The complexity and intricacy of this rich continent makes it even more fascinating.

Americas: Polar opposites

Based on my personal experiences of North, Central and South America, I would be lying if I said that I don't have a favourite.

I absolutely love South America and I would move there tomorrow if I had a valid reason for doing so. Carrying 90 percent bug spray, learning a bit of Spanish and, if visiting Brazil, some Portuguese are essential. With these boxes ticked, you'll have the best time ever.

I met the laziest and happiest animals for the first time in South America: sloths. I was also fortunate to get up close and personal with my ultimate favourite spirit animals: llamas. I love llamas.

My perception of Central America is that it is an extension of South America; full of interesting beaches, islands and volcanoes. I was taken aback by the picturesque landscapes, the passion of the locals and their love for football and culture in both South and Central America. The diversity of many creatures, including insects, and the vast green landscape in Costa Rica was something I never expected.

As for North America, Niagara Falls, Brooklyn Bridge and, obviously, the Empire State Building were my key highlights. I must admit that the lakes in Canada, particularly those in British Columbia and Alberta, are also undeniably breath-taking.

Africa: A Big Deal

Several things about Africa are highly significant for me (aside from the fact that I was born there).

As the second largest continent in the world after Asia, Africa has 55 nations and is home to the largest desert and the longest river* which flows through nine countries in the continent.

The fastest, tallest and largest land animals, as well as the world's largest primate*, are all from Africa.

If you consider yourself a 'tree-hugger', you just love nature, animals and wildlife, or have a direct debit to save the rhino from extinction, this is the continent you should visit.

Being born and raised in Kenya, I'm sure I took safaris for granted during my childhood; I even remember sleeping through some of them. If I think about it now, how often do six-year olds get the opportunity to pat high-spirited lion cubs, play with baby elephants or watch giraffes cross the road?

Africa is a big place, with people who have big hearts; this is a continent that I will always call home.

Sahara Desert; River Nile; Cheetah; Giraffe; African Elephant; Gorilla.

Europe: Small but Mighty

The second smallest continent in the world, but certainly not the weakest.

Home to 44 countries*, of which 12 are still monarchies, and over half of which are still part of the European Union (EU), Europe is the biggest political and economic union in the world.

It's quite remarkable how almost every country in Europe is different in terms of landscapes, sunsets, architecture, languages, cuisine, people, religion, beverages and more.

As you visit the countless museums and observe the diversity of landmarks, you are constantly reminded about the politics, religions and history – including the two World Wars – that have shaped the continent, and how these have affected the people who live there today.

Every church and cathedral I have visited is unique; from the scale of the artwork in St Peter's Basilica in Vatican City, to the quaint little Orthodox Metropolitan church on top of the hill in Fira (or Thira), Santorini.

Walking through the palaces and castles in Europe allow visitors to experience royalty, whether it is Buckingham Palace in London or the Royal Palaces in Brussels and Madrid.

Source: United Nations, 2019

Note: I haven't been to Australia or Antarctica, so I have reserved my views on them for another time.

The Traveller

The growing awareness of the hidden gems in different parts of the world has been accelerated by exposure via television, internet, social media, tourist boards, influencers and world travellers, amongst others. These have all contributed to an increase in the number of people travelling for pleasure.

A global study conducted by the *UNWTO* (*United Nations World Tourism Organisation*) concluded that since the 2008 global financial crisis, there has been a steady increase in the number of travellers around the world.

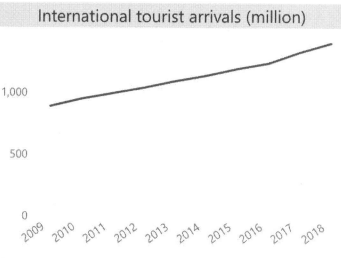

Source: UNWTO.org, 2018 data.

Those with disposable income are increasingly looking at spending more money to create memories and new experiences. This includes investing in travel, rather than in material possessions or potentially both.

People are starting to look for more reasons to step beyond their doorstep and explore the world. Travel is a means of escaping from daily routines, changing lives, relocating, taking time to reflect, discovering more about themselves, growing as a person or just relaxing.

The Hungry Traveller

In today's climate, we know more about what's happening around the world. If we have the choice, more of us want to get out there and explore these places for ourselves.

They say 'travel broadens the mind'; it's true that learning about the lives of other people, both rich and poor, and how they live, the languages they speak, the food they eat, and even how they look, can open our eyes and our minds. Ultimately, this helps us live a more expansive and less judgemental life.

The first step for any potential traveller is to address any issues that holds them back.

Comfort Zones

Comfort
/ˈkʌmfət/ noun
*A state of physical ease and freedom from pain
or constraint.*

Waking up in the comfort of your bed on a Sunday morning
and knowing there's no immediate rush to get up; this is the
best feeling. It's simple and stress-free.

Although we all deserve a nice lie-in, what would be the
consequences of doing that every day?

It's not just about the daily chores we have to perform, but
also the cost of missing new opportunities… if only we had
gotten ourselves out of bed.

Whether going out for a walk, grabbing a coffee (in a
reusable cup of course!), having a nice conversation with
someone over the counter, meeting a friend for a meal or
a drink, these all add to the feeling of having achieved
something that day. Just one or a combination of these
feelings of achievements can give us a boost of joy, or
enhance our feeling of being alive.

We need to give ourselves the chance to experience
something new by negotiating the limits of our comfort
zone, almost on a daily basis.

For a number of reasons, many of us may feel apprehensive
about travelling on our own. Maybe we prefer to have
company, we feel safer or we may feel less likely to miss a
flight or train and so on. We often find comfort in having
someone to rely on.

The Hungry Traveller

For the first two decades of my life, I would naturally choose to holiday with my family and would often wait for friends to align their schedules, finances or horoscopes with mine, in order to go on a trip that would interest me.

Over time, I realised the travel bug had infected me with a less patient wanderlust and I was willing to take the risks linked to breaking out of my comfort zone.

I had to address my fears of the unknown, the responsibility of organisation and the risk of the worst that could happen to me in a foreign place.

There is always the possibility of being robbed, kidnapped (apparently, this is quite possible in Kazakhstan), lose all my money, have no WiFi, or get lost in the middle of nowhere.

After years of procrastinating, I realised that I just had to be positive, have contingency plans in place and pick up some courage to leave my comfort zone.

Going Solo

Lonely
/ˈləʊnli/ adjective
Sad because one is lacking company.

Alone
/əˈləʊn/ adjective
Having no one else present.

For those of you who want to travel alone, but are worried about spending too much time by yourself, it's worth noting the difference between 'feeling lonely' and 'travelling alone'.

It's possible that you might feel lonely whilst travelling solo, but we shouldn't associate the idea of travelling alone with sad experiences.

Travelling with others is obviously the first choice for many of us, because it's more likely to be fun. In many cases, we like conversing, especially on those long journeys and lengthy waits at airports and stations.

As for feeling lonely, that's completely normal when travelling alone. I often start craving interaction with someone, particularly after the fourth consecutive meal alone.

On the other hand, it's also possible to feel lonely when you're travelling with others. From personal experience, I can tell you that travelling with the wrong people can be worse than being alone, especially when you are far from home.

If you have reservations about the idea, my suggestion is to try it at least once, and make informed choices about when to do it, how long for, and in what way – totally by yourself, or with people you don't know (yet). You'll need to consider your needs and ability to adjust.

> *"Making up around 18 percent of global bookings, solo travel is becoming ever more popular and has increased by 7 percent in the last year alone."*

Source: Travelport | October 7, 2019 (phocuswire.com)

City Edit: Stockholm, Sweden
Excerpt from srtravels.co.uk

Having spent the majority of my adulthood in London, one of the busiest cities in the world, Stockholm felt like a yoga retreat.

On a Tuesday evening, I decided to go for a walk to explore Stockholm on my own.

Over the years, I realised that the quickest way to find out the best tourist hotspots is by visiting souvenir shops.

They tend to have a wide coverage of the 'unmissable' landmarks or monuments detailed on a selection of magnets, plates, key rings, tea towels, bags, t-shirts, aprons... you name it, it's there. All probably made in China, but that's not the point.

- ✓ List of places to visit: Done
- ✓ Cheap souvenirs for loved ones back home: Done

So, I followed protocol; I found a souvenir shop, purchased a magnet of a colourful building in Stortorget, the main square of Gamla Stan. This led me to cross a bridge (or four), finally ending up in the cobbled streets of Gamla Stan.

Gamla Stan is not much different to many Old Town squares in Europe. Whilst I could feel a resemblance between Prague, Bruges, Amersfoort and Krakow, Gamla Stan felt really quaint and intriguing.

As I walked into shops and interacted with the locals, I soon realised that every other person I spoke to or saw in Stockholm (excuse the stereotyping), had piercing blue eyes. I am pretty sure I have met more people with blue eyes in three days, than I have in my whole life.

Did You Know...

Swedes have one of the longest life expectancies. This could be due to their relaxed and healthy lifestyle, focusing on quality over quantity and simply the lack of too many people to stress them out.

There's no question that the Nordic countries are on average quite expensive to visit, even more than London. A beer is around GBP 8 (94 Swedish Krona) and at lunchtime, it's normal to spend around GBP 15 (170 Swedish Krona) on a plate of sushi.

Once you get over your empty wallet, you'll appreciate the quality of the food, especially the fish sourced from neighbouring country, Norway. The salmon I ate was probably the smoothest, freshest (and maybe healthiest) I have ever had.

On one occasion, I was enticed by a Spanish restaurant (don't judge me, I did try Swedish food elsewhere) called *The Hairy Pig*. The dim lights and wooden tables created a cosy setting and with such an aura accompanied by delicious tapas-style food and red wine, this was just what I needed to hide away in a corner and watch the world go by.

Having enjoyed an authentic Spanish dinner and sumptuous wine, I took a detour and walked to the harbour near the Old Town. The white boats sat calmly on still water, the silence echoed around the harbour and the sheer absence of people made me feel like I was in a dream.

Finally bored of my own company, I continued to walk until, suddenly, at a distance, I noticed a tower with three golden crowns positioned neatly at the top. I then crossed one of the many bridges to the island where The City Hall stands.

The 106-metre tall tower is part of a much bigger building which was constructed with eight million bricks. I must say that I don't know why anyone would count the number of bricks and I also don't know how many bricks a normal building would have.

With more time and a bigger budget, Stockholm has so much more to offer a visitor; there's a lot to see, whether you choose to enjoy a thirty-minute flight on *FlyOver* or travel via a boat around part of the 60km archipelago, prices ranging from GBP 100 – 200 (1500 to 2500 Swedish Krona).

Unfortunately, I didn't have much time to do either of these activities, or to see many of the other architectural sites the city has to offer, such as the Royal Opera House and the Great Synagogue. Maybe next time.

Fun Facts about Stockholm...

1. Nobel Prizes in Sciences, Literature and Economic Sciences are awarded in the City Hall.
2. Stockholm is the 14th richest city in the world.
3. The famous pop group ABBA was formed in Stockholm in 1972.
4. Stockholm comprises 14 islands and 57 bridges.
5. The city has one of the largest archipelagos (series of islands) in the Baltic sea.

Five Reasons Why You Should Travel Alone (*sometimes*)

Remember your first steps?

Probably not, but the point is that most of you are lucky enough to be able to walk or move. Think of *Bambi*, Disney's little deer and his first attempt (or ten) to stay upright.

When you're travelling alone, especially for the first time, you may have multiple reservations, worries, excuses, negativity – internally and externally.

I'm not suggesting you ignore all the warnings and walk blindly into dangerous situations. A bit of caution and cynicism is good, but not to the point of being unable to take the first step at all.

Reason ONE: Find Yourself

I'm pretty sure you are rolling your eyes as you read this one.

When people say that you will 'find yourself' on your travels, defensive thoughts can sometimes be triggered in your mind. You may think you already know exactly who you are, but the truth is: You don't know what you don't know.

When you travel on your own, you have the time and space to step back from your own life; looking at how things have been so far and think about whether you are where you want to be.

For example, on several occasions, I've returned from a holiday being eighty percent convinced that I should quit the job I was in at the time, to do something cooler, like becoming a scuba instructor.

Who knows, I may become a scuba instructor one day. The main thing is that I explored the idea, and I was able to do so, because I had the time and space to think about it.

You also learn other things about yourself from travelling; which cultures, cuisines, activities and conversations appeal the most and why? What are your limits and what are you willing to forgo if the worst comes to the worst?

Reason TWO: Confidence Boost

Every time you overcome your fears, or do something for the first time, you gain a little bit more confidence in yourself.

As soon as I collected enough Air Miles on my credit card, I booked my first *FREE* return flight to Barcelona. Just with this reward, I felt like I was already winning in life. I know Barcelona is probably one of the safer places to go as a solo traveller, but I was still worried about my accommodation; a hostel room with six bunk beds and the need to converse with strangers for the entire weekend.

At the end of the trip, I returned home feeling more confident about being able to explore a city, chat to strangers and practise my Level 1 Spanish.

Reason THREE: Make New Friends (or at least have a good conversation)

When travelling alone, I do have some of the best conversations with other people. Whether in a pub in Dublin polishing off a full Irish breakfast, including my first experience of white pudding, or while trying to communicate with the locals in non-English speaking countries.

Whilst I wouldn't say I befriended all of those people, I certainly had good conversations.

Reason FOUR: Personal Space

I'm not entirely anti-social, although this book may suggest so on a number of occasions.

Do you feel like you've had enough of humans at times? If you live in a crowded city like me, you may have regular urges to escape from people, including those you actually know and like. Time alone and finding time to enjoy personal space is vital; this period of calm reflection, re-energises your overall well-being.

Some of my friends who have been (un)fortunate enough to travel with me have noticed that there comes a moment, a time or a day or two when I just disappear and start getting a bit cranky. That's when they let me be. Once I've had sufficient time to myself, I'm ready to return to the people I'm travelling with in a much happier mood.

When you finally gain some space, yes, you could be missing out on all the talking, hugging and hand-holding, you might also have the time to read that book you've been wanting to read, but haven't had the time for.

Reason FIVE: Easier Decision Making

What can I have for breakfast?

Ask the jury.

Oh wait, there is no jury. Perfect; I guess I'll eat what I want, wherever I want, whenever I want.

City Edit: Barcelona, Spain
Excerpt from srtravels.co.uk

Eat and drink

First of all, I can't stop eating in Barcelona.

I walked towards Passeig de Gracia and found El Nacional, which has a similar vibe to The Ned in London. Here, you can sit on a bar stool, eye up all the food you want to try and enjoy plenty of cava and tapas. Very fancy, but not expensive at all.

There is a sad side to travelling alone in Barcelona: most restaurants serve paella for two people. So, unless you have a friend, a doggy bag, a massive appetite, or are happy to experience severe guilt from wasting a lot of freshly cooked paella, I suggest visiting places like Santa Anna, not too far from Sagrada Familia, who are willing to make smaller portions of paella for the solo diner.

Night life

During my first visit to Barcelona, my friend and I went to Opium, a club near the beach on La Barceloneta. However, at 10pm, we soon realised that Barcelona does not start partying for, at least, another two hours. We were surrounded by rich people consuming too much shisha for an evening, young adults and some teenage boys trying to chase anything in a skirt. Although the drinks and shisha were very expensive, we were pleased to discover that the tequila shots were not. So, we had tequila all night.

It was definitely a heavy night. At one point, I walked out for fresh air and found myself on the beach; although this was actually quite nice, the club almost didn't let me back in as I didn't have a wrist band (for being one of the losers who showed up 'too early'). The shore and lights curved around the pitch-black sea, blending in with the black sky.

Las Ramblas is the obvious choice for tourists. As the central boulevard at the heart of the city centre, the hustle and bustle of this busy pedestrianised street makes it an enjoyable place to wander around day or night. The appeal of this part of Barcelona can be seen through my three separate visits, each in different circumstances: with my friend, alone and with my dad. The common factor across each visit was that I had a great time on each occasion.

For those looking for luxury, the W hotel is located at the end of the beach and has a rooftop bar with great views across the city. Drinks are not cheap, and it's worth checking the opening days and times as I was once caught out by turning up one afternoon and it was not open until later that evening. Within walking distance from the Gothic quarter and the Picasso museum, several little streets with tapas restaurants and more surround this gem. For those wishing to take in the atmosphere of the city, you can enjoy a pleasant walk, although quite long, or gentle cycle ride along the beach to and from the hotel.

Getting around

Walk (if you can).

You could hire a bike and explore the city at your own pace. Alternatively, the Metro (underground) is relatively easy and cheap to travel on.

Uber is fairly cheap, but not available everywhere.

Buses confuse me, but you could give them a go.

To get to the city centre from the airport, the Airport Bus costs around EUR 6 and I was in town within an hour, with no issues at all. Simply follow the signs at the airport and save yourself some cash.

Where to stay

Staying in a hostel could help you to save more cash; that is if travelling on a budget is important to you. Hostel World can help organise this. However, I do appreciate that not everyone likes the idea of staying in a hostel, but don't be put off. I stayed at Primavera Hostel in the Eixample district, an area buzzing with bars and shops. It's within walking distance of all the tourist spots, and only cost EUR 15 per night.

The hostel itself was very clean, comfortable and homely and if sharing a room with strangers does not appeal, it also offers guests hotel rooms. However, sharing a room with strangers is not such a bad thing; I did enjoy being woken up by someone strumming their guitar and singing a Spanish song... a slight change from the beeping of my daily alarm clock.

Alternatively, most hotels are reasonably priced and often have rooftop pools, which are great during summer. As long as you're staying near a Metro station, reaching the main parts of the city or city centre should be relatively easy.

Languages

I highly recommend learning a bit of Spanish, if you haven't already. Even if the locals look unimpressed when you speak, may not understand what you may be saying, or reply in English, they usually appreciate the effort. Having said that, also be prepared for responses in English if a) like mine, your Spanish isn't the best and/or b) you clearly look like a tourist. Most people in Barcelona seem to speak perfect English anyway.

The Hungry Traveller

What Not to Miss in Barcelona...

1. El Nacional for the variety and atmosphere.
2. Museu Picasso for an overview of his work.
3. Gothic quarter for the ambience and to buy trinkets from the markets. Card payments are also accepted in the markets (which can be useful but also expensive if you wish to shop).
4. Bunkers de Carmel for panoramic views of Barcelona.
5. Experience hostel life.
6. Sagrada Familia for Gaudi's masterpiece.
7. Palau de Musica for a live music performance.
8. Watch Barcelona FC play.
9. Las Ramblas for a night out.
10. La Playa (The Beach).

Fear

Fear
/fɪə/ noun
An unpleasant emotion caused by the threat of danger, pain, or harm.

We all experience different levels of fear at various points in our lives. Sometimes, it's more dramatic and comes from an element of surprise, for instance if you ever walk through a wild forest and are faced by a tiger.

According to WWF (World Wildlife Fund… not the wrestling federation), there were approximately 3,900 tigers left in the world in 2019. So, the reality of that kind of fear is very small.

More realistically, when we travel to a new country, we should be more afraid of humans, than animals. The fear of being robbed or attacked in Caracas, Venezuela is more rational. Regarded as the second most dangerous city in the world, Caracas has a murder rate of 111.2 deaths per 100,000 people (World Population Review, 2019).

However, statistics can always be interpreted. Just because South Africa is the fifteenth most dangerous country in the world, with sixty-two deaths per 100,000 people every year, this hasn't stopped the tourist trade which continues to thrive and have positive reviews.

What if things go wrong?

If we are unfortunate enough to be faced with unforeseen circumstances, we need to have some easy-to-access tools or ideas up our sleeves.

For instance, when I was visiting Antigua in Guatemala, we heard about people on motorbikes snatching bags and, on some occasions, attacking their victims. In Buenos Aires, Argentina, there was a trend of people smearing a smelly, unidentifiable brown paste on tourists' clothes as a form of distraction. While you would try to clean up, they could grab your bag and run away.

When we face danger, whether it's a hungry tiger or a thief, our bodies and minds can react in many ways. This is called a 'Fight-or-Flight' response.

Fight-or-Flight: maintaining calm during crisis situations

Walter Bradford Cannon (1871–1945), a well-known American physiologist, first described this as a physiological reaction that occurs in response to a perceived threat.

Different approaches exist to deal with the response our bodies make before our minds can process things. Here are some tried and tested tips:

1. **Breathe:** try to take a few deep breaths... this might be hard to take seriously, but trust me, even if you take two deep breaths, you'll find you are able to think more clearly, even in dramatic situations.

2. **Poker face:** faking bravery and hiding fear, as well as you can, is very useful. I find that as soon as you show weakness to a potential offender, it could give them a green light to proceed with making you a target.

    Those of you with a natural RBS (Resting-Bitch-Face – please 'Google' it) have an unfair advantage. However, don't worry, those that don't, can practise in front of a mirror.

3. **PMR (Progressive Muscle Relaxation):** this technique, first introduced by Edmund Jacobson, an American physician in the 1930s, involves tightening and releasing major muscles, one at a time. The best thing about this little trick is that no one really notices, and you can carry on with your poker face!

    For instance, clench your fists as tightly as possible for ten seconds, then release. Do this three times and you should feel better.

    PMR is also used for longer term anxiety relief.

Dealing with trauma

If you have already experienced something unpleasant on your trip, especially if you are travelling alone, you need to ensure you don't let that ruin the rest of your holiday or travel plans.

According to *helpguide.org*, here are some ways to deal with a shock or trauma:

- ☐ Allow yourself to feel whatever you're feeling.
- ☐ Give yourself time to feel better.
- ☐ Don't try to rush or force the process.
- ☐ Be patient.
- ☐ Have faith in your abilities to get out of this situation.
- ☐ Be prepared for volatile emotions.
- ☐ Move. Go for a walk, hike, exercise and, if possible, sweat.

This is not an exhaustive list of solutions, but is hopefully a good reminder of how we can take care of ourselves when travelling alone, in groups or just while getting on with life.

FOMO

FOMO
/ˈfəʊməʊ/ noun
Fear Of Missing Out – anxiety that an exciting or interesting event may currently be happening elsewhere, often aroused by posts seen on social media.

In contrast to fear of danger, there's an acronym for being worried about missing out on experiences. This is called FOMO.

Most of us experience a bit of FOMO every now and then, especially from scrolling through social media feeds about how perfect everyone (else) is.

If you experience FOMO of travelling and if you are unable to reprioritise your travels to deal with your FOMO, here are some possible causes and solutions:

1. **Can't leave the country?**

   Make plans to do things where you are; host a party with friends at home, visit museums, start a new hobby.

2. **No time off work?**

   Book some weekend getaways or spa days through websites like *lastminute.com.*

3. **Low on savings?**

   Get yourself a piggy bank. Each time you choose not to buy a coffee, drink, new clothes or something else that you don't really need, put that money into your piggy bank.

   You'll be surprised how much you can save... I once counted GBP 400 after 12 months. Such a good feeling.

4. Just bored?

Avoid using social media or unfollow the accounts that are making you feel like you're missing out. They're probably making it look more fun than it is, anyway.

Article: Inertia
Excerpt from srtravels.co.uk

Inertia

ɪˈnəːʃə / noun
A tendency to do nothing or to remain unchanged.

[Physics] a property of matter by which it continues in its existing state of rest or uniform motion in a straight line, unless that state is changed by an external force.

You'll be pleased to know that this article is not about Galileo or Isaac Newton's Law of Motion (unless, you actually liked Physics in school, then you may be disappointed!)

Many of us resist change. We get used to our lives being on 'autopilot'. This could be because we prefer not to venture too far beyond our comfort zones, we just don't like the uncertainty of unfamiliar territory, or we start to feel like we are losing control over situations, routines, or even our lives.

When things change

Adjusting to change in your life can be disruptive. Your job changes, your best friend starts dating someone slowly putting an end to your regular nights out, you change schools, you become a parent, you get married, or divorced, someone leaves you, or you leave them, you relocate, or someone close to you relocates; all of these events impact us, as individuals, in different ways and can require additional mental and physical effort. Not knowing what to expect or do after periods of change can lead to the temptation to resist it all and simply cling on to what we already have or know.

Personally, I hate change and avoid it like the plague, but over the years, whether it's happened voluntarily or involuntarily, I've learnt one thing: change is a learning process. Whatever happens, we can find something new to learn from our experience, if we look hard enough.

1. Learn about ourselves

When things change, we can learn more about ourselves and how we manage our emotions and situations during such times.

Sometimes, even I am unhappy with my own behaviour when dealing with change. At times like this, I find most comfort when I speak to trusted sources, such as close friends, family or mentors.

Even when it's difficult, I believe that when we come through change, however challenging, our endurance, mental strength and ability to deal with future change improves.

From a personal development point of view, change can be a blessing in disguise.

2. Learn about others

Change can also teach us a few things about others.

Sometimes, it can be a test of our relationships with, and our understanding of, other people, including those we think we know very well. Someone you barely know could come and save your life or help you during times of change or difficulty. Alternatively, someone you think you know well could either help you when you need them, or disappear and disappoint.

We can't control how others behave and feel about us, but events and changes can make us learn more about the people in our lives.

3. Opportunities

Change can also be exciting.

It can open doors to new opportunities and experiences, expanding your own personal growth in ways that you'd never have imagined.

"I believe that everything happens for a reason. People change so that you can learn to let go, things go wrong so that you appreciate them when they're right, you believe lies so you eventually learn to trust no one but yourself, and sometimes good things fall apart so better things can fall together."

— *Marilyn Monroe*

However, we can't ignore the fact that not all changes are good or work out well for everyone.

Fundamentally, we can be hit by almost any situation, at any time. It's, therefore, more important to think about how we, as individuals, handle situations of change.

Many situations can test us. If someone close to us is taken seriously ill; or if we lose our job and have nowhere to live; or we are stranded in the middle of a holiday in an unfamiliar country. Appreciating how any of those things could ever have a positive impact or outcome can be hard to see when you're in a challenging situation.

In such situations, we should remind ourselves to:

1. Be positive (to motivate us and those affected).
2. Evaluate the situation, sometimes at lightning speed, if it's an emergency.
3. Find a practical solution and back up options to move forward and choose from.
4. Make important decisions.
5. Be patient.

I can tell you that some of the most memorable things I've personally experienced in my life so far, have been either a trigger for change, or as a result of change.

Building Courage

Courage
/ˈkʌrɪdʒ/ noun
The ability to do something that frightens one; bravery.

Fear of loss.
Fear of danger.
Fear of failure.

What moves us forward is the ability to build up courage to address, rather than fight, that fear.

In terms of travelling, or challenging ourselves physically and mentally, the first thing that may come to mind could be anything from "I don't think I can do it" to "I'm not fit enough" or "I'm not experienced enough". Depending on what 'enough' actually means to you or those around you, it is possible that you aren't fit enough or experienced enough; however, this can be changed.

Do your research, prepare yourself with more knowledge or training, create a plan of action, and provide yourself with the toolkit to improve your confidence and courage. You will increase your belief in your ability to *try* to complete a challenge, or at least, bring it to life after a solo trip.

In short, build your own courage and learn to ignore all the negative chatter from your mind and from others.

At times, when I tell some people about my next adventure, I expect someone to come up with a scare story. In such cases, it is important to understand that most of the time, people don't do this out of jealousy (although on occasion, some might). It is more said out of concern for your safety and a hope that you'll manage your expectations and be adequately prepared for all eventualities.

Example 1: Before my trip to Honduras,
Central America:

*"I heard someone's hands got chopped off last month
in Honduras."*

Example 2: Before attempting to climb
Mount Kilimanjaro:

*"My friend caught pneumonia and almost died when
he tried to climb it."*

If I had decided not to visit either of these places based on
what others said, I would not have had the memories of
the Copán Ruinas, a unique archaeological site of the Maya
civilisation or woken up above the clouds at the highest
point in Africa.

Therefore, I urge you to make your own informed choices
based on your own research, not just hearsay. Prepare
yourself to the best of your abilities.

Organised Tours

The alternative to organising your own trips is to let others do the hard work for you. I am naturally quite an emotionally-lazy person. So, if there's a chance something can involve less or minimal mental effort from me to achieve the desired outcome, I will, in most cases, choose that option.

Therefore, when choosing a multi-destination holiday with an organised group tour, my natural choice was to go through tour companies, such as *G Adventures, Tucan Travel,* or *Intrepid.*

When I am lacking time or even lacking the funds, selecting from a range of tours to see the key highlights of a location can be a smart choice. It's like a crash course in the world. If you really like a particular place, you can always consider returning there for a longer visit in the future.

For those of you who are more independent (or anti-social), you can always choose tours that give you free days for you to do your own thing. Having said that, many organised tours have an element of flexibility, especially in terms of meals.

Feeling Anti-social?

Depending on how sociable you want to be during your time off, you may need to consider if you want to hang out with a group of people you've never met, and for how long.

One week with a group of people you don't get along with is much more bearable than three weeks with them. I've seen first-hand how initial hesitations and reserved personalities, including myself, have exposed themselves over the course of some of these trips.

Before booking an organised tour, just remind yourself that people come in all shapes and sizes, backgrounds, mannerisms, personalities, experiences, judgements and more. Sometimes, we just have to deal with it.

Age

My first organised tour was when I was twenty-five. We travelled across Brazil, Uruguay and Argentina and up to that point, it was, by far, the best trip of my life.

Our experience on a party boat was memorable for sure, even though the cocktails made the memories slightly hazy. As soon as our party boat left the shore at 10am in the morning, we drank *caipirinhas*, made from *cachaça*, fermented sugar cane juice, from large plastic buckets. This continued until the evening. We swam to islands around Paraty in Brazil, dived off cliffs, admired the hills, the sunset, the reflections on the sea and shared our declarations of undying love for each other. The group of twenty- and thirty-somethings were in-sync with each other and we all had a great time. Of course, being honest, there were exceptions to this but we don't need to discuss them.

As I moved further away from my twenties (sad face) and into my thirties, I realised how much I struggle to keep up with the youth of today.

A few years later, I went on another organised tour across South East Asia. The consecutive days of partying and drinking that my dewy skinned travel buddies were capable of, was exhausting. It was something that no longer appealed to me.

Early bird or lie-in lover?

Sometimes, you'll be asked to wake up ridiculously early for various reasons, hangover or not, such as watching the sun rise from Angkor Wat in Cambodia, or just catching the earlier train because you chose the cheaper tour.

If you prefer a lie-in on your holidays, you may wish to look further into their itineraries in more detail, or reconsider. Alternatively, you can practise sleeping on buses, boats, trains and the floor to make up your hours of sleep, if necessary.

Who are you travelling with?

If you're travelling alone, I would recommend these tours as you'll probably make friends, have people to play board games with or *Cards Against Humanity* or *UNO* with and often, there are other solo travellers in the group, who are in the same position as you.

I've met both friendly and unfriendly couples on some tours. If you are the latter (be honest), it may be worth reconsidering organised tours.

For those travelling with family, there are family-friendly tours. However, it's worth looking into the daily itinerary to see if it works for babies, children, elderly members of the family and so on.

Location

If you are going to a location which is considered slightly dangerous, like Honduras, in Central America and/or if you don't speak the local language, having a tour and a tour leader to help you navigate safely can be a good way to see a place you might be apprehensive about visiting previously.

On the other hand, if you're planning to go somewhere like South East Asia, which is very tourist-friendly and cheap, it makes more sense to go on your own.

Diet

Vegans, vegetarians and those with other specific dietary needs may wish to check the flexibility of the meal options with the tour operators.

What's included?

It's important to see exactly what activities, meals, transportation and accommodation are included in the price you pay to the tour operators. There have been times when I've had to pay quite a lot of additional money in each place I visited with the tour group, in order to get the "full experience". Once you're there, it's usually a good idea to just go for it, or else you may suffer from serious FOMO.

Reviews

I know many people complete reviews when they are emotional or angry about a negative experience, but I'd like to believe that many also give positive feedback when well-deserved. It's worth double checking the reviews for some of the hotels and tours on comparison websites, with that in mind.

Going Out

When you decide to travel with others, whether you're planning to party with your friends or new travel buddies, there are some places where the night life can be buzzing, while in others it's non-existent.

For instance, Ataco, in El Salvador, Central America, was entirely asleep by nine in the evening and five of us walked back to our hotel in disappointment.

Here are five cities where I've had some of the best evenings out:

1. **Bangkok, Thailand**

    Bangkok has been known for all sorts of parties, but it's redeemed its image for the wider public.

    Buy yourself a *Chang* beer t-shirt or vest, walk down Khao San Road after having visited all the temples (Don't miss: Wat Pho, Wat Arun, Golden Temple), then head to a rooftop bar to enjoy the night skyline of Thailand's capital city.

    There are dress codes to comply with in certain bars, such as restrictions about flip-flops, shorts, vests or trainers, sometimes you need to wear a shirt. However, I advise that it is often worth scrubbing up for.

    Favourite:

    Lebua (The Hangover Bar): Bangkok, Thailand
    Price: $$$

    I can confirm that this bar has the best open-air panoramic views of Bangkok.

The cocktails were as good as expected (at that price); the magical feeling, when you're having a martini high above the city, while a pianist plays, elevated on a separate platform, as if they were in the sky. This experience is priceless; just make sure you forget about the actual price you paid for the drink.

2. Buenos Aires, Argentina

Malbec-lovers, you are home!

The day I landed, I joined a random group of people for a late dinner with a stereotypical amazing Argentinian steak and a glass of their local Malbec wine. If that wasn't enough for the perfect start to my holiday, we soon discovered that almost every street in the area of Palermo has a bar, club or restaurant.

Buenos Aires is known for its *boliches* (nightclubs), many of which are in warehouses or old restored theatres. For a more mystic experience, you could even watch the sunrise from the clubs in Río de la Plata. This is ideal for those who are able to power through the night.

Favourite:

Boticario: Buenos Aires, Argentina
Price: $

Cheap and authentic, so why not. With ferns flowing down from the floor above and one side decorated to look like a wooden cabinet, it's one of those places that really makes you smile as you walk towards it.

3. Barcelona, Spain

I quite enjoyed starting the evening with *croquetas* and *cerveza* at a number of little tapas restaurants at Las Ramblas. We then ended up at a beach-front club called Opium. Other popular places include Razzmatazz, with five floors of unique themes and, sometimes, even live music; Heliogàbal, a place for artists and live music.

The Barcelona clubbing scene doesn't really kick-off until after midnight. So, for those who fancy a nap after their meal, before going out, it is definitely advisable.

For a more low-key evening, you could head to one of the live Spanish guitar shows. However, if you like to combine the best of music, food and beer, you can head to places like Bar Pastis, a small and charming venue with classy cocktails while you enjoy the performances.

Favourite:

Paradiso: Barcelona, Spain
Price: €€

Remember the last time you casually walked through a pastrami freezer door and entered a cocktail bar? Although it's increasingly common for bars with such 'surprises', this is quite a pleasant find, especially as the creativity continues into the colour-changing, disappearing cocktails. Enough to keep you entertained all night long. *Uno más por favor*!

4. London, UK

As someone who lives in London, I'm spoilt for choice in terms of nightlife, be it wine bars, jazz bars, cocktail bars, and nightclubs from mainstream to celebrity hang-outs, salsa parties to Bollywood disco nights. The only thing to keep in mind is the dent in your wallet afterwards.

I love a good cocktail on a night out and if you do too, here are five of my personal favourites in the city*.

Based on personal visits made in 2019, considering the quality of the cocktail(s) consumed, uniqueness of ambience and service.

I. Merchant House, Well Court
Price: £££

Cosy underground bar that feels like a fancy living room owned by someone rich, with wooden furniture, a grandfather clock, stuffed real animals (not sure about those…) and bespoke cocktails made by people who almost know too much about alcohol and mixology.

II. Mr Fogg's House of Botanicals, Newman Street
Price: ££

This is one of the bars in the Mr & Mrs Fogg's collection based on Jule Verne's novel *Around the World in 80 Days*.

The place is mostly white, with comfortable sofas and settees with plants hanging everywhere.

The presentation of the cocktails is pretty special, but the volume of the cocktails could certainly be more.

III. Blixen Bar III, Spitalfields
Price: ££

This one wins on the service and the small, dimly lit corners that resemble caves, cushioned seats and sofas, giving every group or person some privacy.

The classic cocktails are on the money. They monitor how many people are present so it's never overly busy or noisy.

This is my current favourite.

IV. City Social, Old Broad Street
Price: ££££

In principle, because of how ridiculously expensive the drinks are here, I shouldn't have added this to my list. However, I think the classic cocktails are probably the best I've had.

Plus, there's the stunning view of London from the twenty-fourth floor to consider...

V. Kwãnt, Heddon Street
Price: £££

Hidden under a North African restaurant (Momo), the lounge takes you to another era, with smooth and perfectly balanced cocktails.

It's very relaxing but try not to fall asleep.

"The bar takes you back to 1940s classic Casablanca, just with better drinks and a bit more colour." (Worldsfiftybestbars.com, 2019)

5. **Lima, Peru**

This is an unconventional choice, as the place
you might think of when I say 'party' and 'South
America' is probably Rio de Janeiro. However,
to me, Lima might be the underdog. It has
more romantic and chilled vibes; it's not all
about parties.

From relaxed cocktail bars, to watching a
performance of the Marinera, an elegant dance
representing courtship and love, to full-on
nightclubs like Tequila Rock, Lima has something
for the lazy and the active. Most night clubs are in
the areas of Miraflores and Barranco.

Favourite:

Ayahuasca: Lima, Peru
Price: $$

This place took me by surprise, to the point that
I couldn't stop walking around the building. The
more I walked, inside and outside, I saw another
hidden area. Every room had a different vibe, one
with Peruvian rugs rolled into glass jars, another
with a few rocking chairs and couches, another
with a modern bar, and then an outside area
which was actually a glorified dancefloor.

To encourage me to explore more, I tried plenty of
varieties of *pisco sours*, a drink based on a type of
brandy produced in winemaking regions of Peru
and Chile, originating in the 16th century.

Before You Travel

Visas

Before you start getting excited about the new countries that you'll be adding to your list of countries visited (admit it, you do count), look up whether you need a visa based on your passport. It is important to be aware whether online applications are required for e-Visas and if *visa on arrival* is possible at your destination airports.

It's worth knowing that the Schengen states ask for an Airport Transit Visa. This is needed by passport-holders of a number of countries just to travel via their airports – even if you don't step outside the building.

Also, don't forget to check if you need a single-entry or multiple-entry visa before applying.

Passport

To avoid having a rejected application or even being rejected entry into a number of countries, always check whether you have at least two full empty pages on your passport.

Most places also ask for a minimum of six months of validity of your passport, from the date of your flight, before allowing you to travel into the country.

Travel & Medical Insurance

Depending on the type of trip you're going on, you should ensure that you have insurance cover for the more likely events, such as missed flight connections and lost baggage with no (or a small sum of) excess charged.

In terms of medical cover, it is important to check what the in-patient claim rules are, the excess, and whether they cover existing health conditions.

If you are planning to take part in adventure sports, such as sky diving, skiing, racing, or hiking above 5000m of altitude, and if you're doing anything non-leisurely, it's worth checking the documents to ensure you're covered if anything happens to you during those activities.

Don't forget to check that your insurance covers all the continents you plan to visit. Before you travel, make a note of the emergency numbers and your policy numbers.

If possible, carry a printed copy of the policies and keep them separate from your passport and other documents. With modern-day technology, I'm sure you can save a copy of it somewhere on a Cloud or your mobile.

Accommodation

Write down the address of the place where you're staying, just in case your phone battery dies, to show your taxi or bus driver. If you're super-organised, you could even print out the directions from the airport to the accommodation.

Extra cash

My bank cards have been eaten by ATMs in at least four different countries. This is when having some spare cash, such as USD which is a universally accepted currency, and an extra bank card (or even a good friend) is a smart move. Keeping them in different places, say one in your wallet and the other in another bag, is even smarter, in case you lose one or the other.

Taxi-App

I don't know if Uber will be around forever, and with my 4.75 rating I can say that I have warm and cold feelings about it.

There have been plenty of times when I've ended up in a city, whether Copenhagen, Frankfurt, London, Stockholm or Kolkata, when Uber has saved me a lot of the stress of trying to find a taxi or an alternative mode of transport or even just waiting or walking around for ages.

There are plenty of other taxi companies expanding their network globally, such as Ola, Careem, Lyft, Gett and Taxify. So, the customer has more choice about their taxi provider; you can take your pick and download the relevant app on your phone.

For safety, it is advisable to take a photo of the registration plate of the car you are getting into and send it to someone, especially in unknown destinations.

Medications & Vaccinations

Don't forget to check whether your medications are legal in the countries you plan to visit. Understanding which vaccines are also required before entering specific countries is essential.

When I travelled to a number of countries in Africa and South and Central America, I needed a Yellow Fever certificate to travel. This definitely wasn't cheap… around GBP 50; however, it was necessary.

Embassy

In case of emergencies, it is important to keep the number of your local Embassy to hand. If anything was to happen, such as being robbed and losing your passport, you may have to reach out to them for help.

Note: this is not an exhaustive list. You should do your own research to ensure you have everything you need before you travel.

Article: Lessons from Strangers
Excerpt from srtravels.co.uk

Stranger
/ˈstreɪn(d)ʒə noun
Someone with whom one is not familiar.

The word stranger could have a negative aura. However, in fact, it's a very neutral word.

Here are some instances when a stranger, or someone I met for the first time, said something to me that I found useful long after we met.

1. **Immigration Officer**

   In my mind, I was busy replaying how I'd said 'Bonjour' to the Immigration Officer at the Eurostar terminal in Paris, when he looked at me and asked:

   "Did you know your name means Traveller?"

   Putting aside the minor identity crisis from discovering that my given name [Sanchari] has another meaning, I guess this piece of new information wasn't far from reality.

2. **Lady on the train**

   A lady decided to strike up a conversation with me on the train home. If you're a Londoner, you'll know how uncomfortable this makes us feel. We don't talk to strangers.

   She was incredibly bubbly and chatty, so I didn't mind. Just before she got off the train, she said:

   "Don't rush anything."

I honestly have no idea where this came from, as she did most of the talking, but it stayed with me.

Whether it's while climbing mountains like Ben Nevis in Scotland or Mount Kilimanjaro in Tanzania, or in relationships, careers or health and fitness, this is an absolutely priceless piece of simple advice.

As humans, we are conditioned to feel like everything is a race. Achievement feels great and it is important for a sense of fulfilment.

However, it's always worth taking regular breaks to re-evaluate and consider your long-term goals. Enjoy the view while you walk up that mountain, don't rush it.

3. Lady at Ojo de Agua, Ometepe Island in Nicaragua

We finally made it to the natural volcanic pool we were looking for. I should hope so after the effort we made; cycling for over twenty kilometres on clunky metallic bikes, in over thirty degrees heat, with intermittent downpours of torrential rain.

When reaching for a coconut water, a lady stopped me and said:

"Don't have that, have the Coco Loco..."

That was still the same coconut, minus half of the coconut water, plus a generous portion of rum. I listened to her and before I knew it, after around five Coco Locos, we were having a full-on conversation about *life*.

To be honest, I don't remember anything from that conversation, except that we concluded:

"No preconceptions."

To put this in context, we mutually decided that we should (try) not to have ready-made opinions or conclusions about people, places or even endeavours in life before we get to know more about them, over time.

In short, let us try to be less 'judgey'.

Like most people, I judge almost instantly, but very often I have been wrong.

Did You Know...

Ometepe Island is one of many islands in Nicaragua in Central America. The water in Ojo de Agua comes directly from the Concepción Volcano. It contains magnesium, calcium, sulphur and sodium, which are known to help with muscular pain and stress.

The pools have a constant temperature of 24-26°C (75-79°F), a depth of minimum 50 cm and maximum 3.50 m.

You can also find some monkeys and turtles to hang out with, while you're there.

Challenges & Limits

We have two choices in life: to live actively or reactively.

Active: face your fears, take initiative, challenge yourself.

Reactive: live in a bubble, avoiding risks, remaining in your comfort zones.

Those of us who are more 'active' in this sense, may need or prefer constant challenges to remain motivated in life. It's important to be aware that you can become addicted to challenging yourself. There's a difference between a need and an obsession and it's healthier to keep on the right side of that line. You don't want to be caught in a cycle of constantly needing to have your next challenge lined up.

We need to be comfortable with the gap between our challenges and achievements and accept the occasional 'lull' in life and it's important to be content in either situation.

We need to find a balance between trying to learn more about ourselves and just how much we should push our limits.

Challenges test our mental strength as much as our physical strength but, sometimes they can push us to our breaking point.

However, my own experience is that these times of struggle can bring us closer to our companions in the challenges, whether they are our friends, family or strangers.

Sometimes, challenges can bring us closer to our own thoughts, helping us understand how we can push ourselves beyond our preconceived 'limits'.

Here are FOUR reasons why you should challenge yourself once in a while:

Reason ONE: It builds on your self-confidence.

After every challenge you overcome, you are likely to feel a sense of contentment. A little bit of pride in your hard work, struggles and accomplishments is not a terrible thing.

Reason TWO: Makes you learn how to deal with failure.

Let's face it, we can't complete every challenge in our lives. So, when we don't, it helps us learn how to manage our emotions, look at the positive side and realise what we have gained from it.

Reason THREE: You increase your 'limits'.

Challenges are meant to push our limits and test our patience. In situations where we are massively outside our comfort zones, we can find new ways of improving our strategies, and priorities, finding motivation in them.

Reason FOUR: You're less bored.

I do get bored. When I do, I have to come up with some good (and bad) ideas for the next thing I want to do to challenge myself. I write them down, and refer to the list once in a while, until I decide to make time and act on it.

Challenges I would recommend...

1. Hang-gliding in Rio de Janeiro, Brazil.
2. Skiing in Andorra la Vella, Andorra.
3. Camping in Okavango Delta, Botswana.
4. Canyoneering (Canyoning) in the Lost Canyon, Costa Rica.
5. Kayaking in Nam Song River, Laos.
6. Trekking in Ausangate (Rainbow Mountains), Peru.
7. Undersea walking in Port Luis, Mauritius.
8. Quad biking in Santorini, Greece.
9. White water rafting in River Zambezi, Zimbabwe.
10. Motorbike riding in Hue, Vietnam.

Challenge: Kilimanjaro, Tanzania
Excerpt from srtravels.co.uk

Step 1: Deciding

You need to ask yourself a few questions before you decide
to climb Mount Kilimanjaro:

- Does the idea of camping and not showering for
  days upset you?
- Are you afraid of heights?
- Do you get bored after walking for a few hours?
- Do you run out of breath easily?
- Have you saved some money for flights, an
  organised tour, equipment, visas, accommodation
  and training?
- Why do you want to climb Mount Kilimanjaro?
- Who would you climb it with? Or would you
  go solo?

Step 2: Choosing a route

This will depend on what's more important to you. For
instance, if you hate camping, the 'Coca-Cola' route
(Marangu) is the most touristy one of them all, with
cabin accommodation.

Here are the main routes to the top of the mountain:

1. Marangu
2. Machame
3. Lemosho
4. Shira
5. Rongai (this is the one I did)
6. Northern Circuit
7. Umbwe

Step 3: Packing checklist

- ☐ Waterproof socks (SmartWool)
- ☐ High calorie snacks
- ☐ Contacts / glasses
- ☐ Fleece jacket
- ☐ Down jacket
- ☐ Thermal tights
- ☐ Gloves inners
- ☐ Gloves waterproof
- ☐ Diamox (for altitude sickness; please note the side-effects of this as well)
- ☐ Dry shampoo
- ☐ Toothpaste & toothbrush
- ☐ AAA batteries x6 (for the flashlights)
- ☐ Baby and antibacterial wipes (several days without a shower or a real toilet... you will need wipes)
- ☐ Pocket money (for tipping the porters)
- ☐ Solar charger backpack
- ☐ First aid kit and paracetamol
- ☐ Rain jacket
- ☐ Gaiters (to keep trousers dry)
- ☐ T shirts
- ☐ Quick dry towel
- ☐ Backpack 70l
- ☐ Rucksack 30–40l
- ☐ Balaclava (for icy cold winds... or just wind... or if you would like to rob the neighbouring tent)
- ☐ Woolly hat
- ☐ Waterproof cover for your backpacks
- ☐ Walking poles
- ☐ Underwear
- ☐ Hairbrush
- ☐ Travel insurance (needs to cover up to 6000m)
- ☐ Passport
- ☐ Sunglasses
- ☐ Book or Kindle

- ☐ Waterproof phone case
- ☐ Earphones
- ☐ Speaker
- ☐ Mobile phone
- ☐ Camera
- ☐ Chargers & Battery packs
- ☐ Thermal tops
- ☐ Hydration bladder
- ☐ Hydration salts
- ☐ Nail clipper
- ☐ Nail polish (to hide all the dirt)
- ☐ Sunscreen
- ☐ Lip balm
- ☐ Deodorant
- ☐ Moisturiser
- ☐ Convertible trekking pants (shorts/trousers)
- ☐ Merino wool jumper(s)
- ☐ Hiking boots (waterproof, sometimes better as one size bigger)
- ☐ Open sandals
- ☐ Water bottle
- ☐ Laundry bags
- ☐ Sleeping bag liner
- ☐ Sleeping bag and mattress
- ☐ Head torch
- ☐ Toilet paper
- ☐ Hot water bottle
- ☐ Vodka – to warm your insides after the trek... just a sip!
- ☐ Money belt (more for wipes, sanitiser) for those midnight trips to the toilet tent (a portable toilet inside a tent... don't forget your head torch...)

Step 4: Training

The success rate is around sixty-five percent, in terms of getting to the 'summit', depending on which route you take (*climbkilimanjaroguide.com*, 2018).

At 5,895m height, most of the advice I read on various blogs suggested that the trick is in walking slowly, acclimatising, practising with long walks for two to three months before the trek.

I was aiming to train three times a week, for at least one hour per session, at a minimum. It's recommended that day hikes for four to six hours take place, ideally in places with an element of change in elevation and even altitude, while carrying a 10kg pack. I didn't do this, but, upon reflection, I probably should have.

Your longest and hardest workouts should be performed two to four weeks before your departure. During the last two weeks, training should taper off and in the final days, rest is essential to allow the body time to recover before the actual climb. In addition to walking or hiking, you can also supplement your training with exercises, such as running or cycling, which will increase your aerobic capacity.

Step 5: Don't panic

You should certainly read a few blogs from those who have climbed Mount Kilimanjaro. Write down what's important; packing, diet, exercise, pacing yourself, the right clothing and equipment, medications, insurance for over 5800m altitude, luggage weight limits, portable toilets and tipping porters. Then, build up on your positive attitude and ignore everything else.

Some people have climbed Mount Kilimanjaro in two days, while others take eight days.

Just work on your positive spirit, prepare as best as possible, be practical and sensible and go for it, without fear of 'failing'.

What actually happened?

Four of us walked and breathed slowly, monitoring our heartbeats, sipping water and Diarolyte in our hydration bladders. We got used to putting our jackets on and then taking them off very frequently.

There were thirteen porters and three guides to accompany us for the five days.

We made it to Kibo Hut i.e. the base camp at 4700m above sea level, from where the night trek to the summit starts on day five.

We were fed four (freshly cooked) meals a day with plenty of carbs and protein, thanks to our tour company. We ate to our hearts' content every single day, which was amazing.

On 'summit night', we wore five layers on top, covered our heads and faces, wore 'gaiters' for the snow on top of the mountain and headed off with our head lamps (a must) "pole pole" (meaning: slowly slowly). 1km up the slopes on the summit night felt like 10km to me. Sadly, I had to turn back to the base camp as I couldn't breathe and had to sleep in the freezing cold tent in all my layers.

But despite the cold nights and having to go to the toilet at 4 am, the night sky lit by the moonlight and hundreds of stars, waking up above the clouds in bright sunlight (you need a lot of sunscreen to avoid getting sun burn... even if you're dark skinned) is totally worth it.

Oh, and due to the cold weather, there were no insects (hurrah!).

TIPS:

- *A hot water bottle will be your best friend at night.*
- *You need to use walking poles, especially on the last day of walking downhill for up to nine hours.*
- *Wear knee braces on the last day or they will hurt... a lot (carry Ibuprofen anyway).*
- *You need a balaclava, no matter how horrendous you may look wearing one (a friend called me a 'blue worm')*
- *Contact lenses can crack at the top of the mountain (temperatures can go down to -15 degrees Celsius).*
- *Your shins and the back of your shoulders will get burnt unless you wear sunscreen.*
- *Carry baby wipes and antibacterial spray at all times.*
- *A Go-PRO (or a cheaper substitute) in a waterproof case will be useful if it rains or in snow.*
- *You'll probably wear the same clothes for most of the trek... and you'll be fine! I wore normal gym clothes and a rain jacket for 6 days.*

Overall, it was a once in a lifetime experience. The main thing I learnt from the trip is that it's the journey as well as the destination that makes it unforgettable.

Favourite memory: waking up above the clouds.

10 Things for your Eco-friendly Travel Kit

1. **Reusable water bottle**

   Whether you're in hot or cold weather conditions, instead of buying or consuming water from several plastic bottles of water, you could carry one of these.

   There are plenty of BPA-free bottles out there to choose from.

   Thermos flasks are now much smaller and handier than before. You can keep some hot tea for those colder days to sip over a long period of time, or cold water for scorching hot conditions.

   Hydration packs produced by brands like *CamelBak* are designed for longer treks, biking and other outdoor activities, with more capacity than a water bottle (1.5 to 3 litres).

2. **Packing cubes made from recycled plastic bottles**

   Along with making it easier to fit more things into your bag, recycled plastic cubes are also doing something about all the other plastic that has been thrown away in the past.

   These are made of recycled polyester (RPET) fabric, which is derived from recycling post-consumer plastic bottles. Win-win-win.

3. **Kinetic watch**

   This is more of a long-term choice of time-keeping and fashion. They work through the energy generated while the watch is worn on your wrist, which is stored in a storage unit (Kinetic ESU) – so you'll never have to buy or replace a battery for the watch.

4. **Antibacterial and odourless socks**

   Bye smelly feet.

   These socks have an infusion of silver, copper, and zinc, which work to kill bacteria that accrues from wearing the socks all day. Fewer bacteria means less smelly feet.

5. **Organic cotton t-shirts**

   Amongst many other producers of organic clothing, there's a company called *The Cotton Story*. Recommended by my friend, I purchased half a dozen t-shirts over the course of a few months.

   Apart from the fact that they are super comfortable and soft, their production needs less water and is generally cheaper and more environmentally friendly.

   They are also more likely to be good for people with sensitive skin or allergies.

6. **Eco-friendly, quick dry towel**

I use these in the gym, so that I don't have to worry about carrying a damp towel around in my bag for long periods of time.

Pandoo is a company selling eco-friendly towels made from nylon and 40 percent bamboo-activated carbon fibres. They are light and quick-drying, as well as hypoallergenic.

7. **Solar-power battery charger**

Some of the cheaper solar battery packs are pretty useless.

It may be a bit of an investment initially, but if you get a sturdy one with a decent power storage of above 20,000 m, then you can rely on it for longer outdoors excursions.

I used the *ANKER* solar charger on my longer treks, which charged my phone several times. However, they are heavy and bulky.

8. **Natural Deodorant**

Another friend recommended the Charcoal Natural Deodorant Balm from Holland & Barrett.

This uses 'activated charcoal' for extra odour absorption and has baking soda which helps to absorb wetness and neutralise odour. I found it easy to apply and quick-drying.

9. Bamboo everything

Bamboo based items can be found in many forms: cotton buds, toothbrushes, pens, cutlery, bags and even towels and clothes. They're not expensive and are in high supply. A major advantage is that they are 100 percent biodegradable.

Don't worry, bamboo roots remain in place after harvesting and take around four years to grow back, compared to normal trees which could take over 25 years. This means that we can use bamboo products guilt-free.

10. O-free Sunscreen

Hawaii has banned skincare companies from selling sunscreen that contain oxybenzone and octinoxate on its islands. The main reason for this is the damage it causes to its marine life.

Apparently, around 25 percent of the sunscreen ingredients we apply end up in the water.

Source: Independent.co.uk

City Edit: Zakopane, Poland
Excerpt from srtravels.co.uk

We walked for nine hours on our first day of trekking the Tatra Mountains, a *UNESCO* site shared by the Polish and Slovakians. We didn't climb the 2500m to one of the peaks, but we did get to around 1800m, where we enjoyed a warm, fruity ginger beer.

During our climb, we noticed that the weather and the time of year caused the lakes to appear slate-coloured. Another hiker showed us photos from a day earlier, where the lakes were more turquoise in colour.

The best thing we did was to carry freshly baked chocolate cake from the bakery that morning. In addition, we had a reusable hot water bottle with our favourite tea, as well as layers and rainproof covers for our backpacks and ourselves.

The following day, we went to Koscielisko Valley in the Western side of Tatra National Park. This was an 'easier' trek, passing through forests, seeing streams and waterfalls and a secluded lake. We then decided to check out the caves. We thought this would involve strolling into a cave, taking a few photos and walking out. Instead, it involved close-to-vertical climbs and descents on soap-textured rocks, using nothing but a metal chain and a lot of arm strength.

This wasn't quite the same as indoor bouldering, where you would fall on a mattress; or canyoneering where you are clipped onto all sorts of things to make sure you will, at least, hang in the middle of nowhere, rather than falling into a valley never to be seen again. It was very scary, but at the end of the day, I had a great sense of achievement of staying alive.

What not to miss in Poland...

1. Vodka: Soplica
2. Dumplings
3. Oscypek: smoked sheep's milk cheese
4. Chocolate: Wawel
5. Sausages

Nature

Ecotherapy
ˈiːkəʊθɛrəpi/ noun

Exposure to nature and the outdoors as a form or component of psychotherapy.

According to nutrition expert, Katie Wells, Founder and CEO of Wellness Mama, 'ecotherapy' is an actual human need.

Some of the main benefits of going out into nature, whether near home or somewhere far away, include:

1. **Better sleeping patterns**

   If you sleep well, your immune system works better. Therefore, you are more likely to live a healthier and longer life.

2. **Better mental health**

   Regular exposure to nature is more likely to result in fewer symptoms of stress, anxiety and/or depression, whether it's from sun light or fresh air.

   Fresh air can be a good source of negative ions, also known as 'nature's antidepressants'. You can get your negative ions outside, especially near a beach or waterfalls.

3. **Better physical health**

   It's believed that those who spend time hiking or even relaxing on a hammock in a forest are more likely to have lower blood pressure.

Did you know...

Vitamin D deficiency has been linked to obesity and some forms of cancer and weaker bones. Sunshine is the primary source of Vitamin D and mental wellbeing for many.

In Peru, *Intihuatana* means 'to tie the sun', where leaders would traditionally spend the Winter Solstice praying to the Sun to bless the community with good harvests.

When I go to the beach, I react a bit like Rowan Atkinson in *Mr Bean's Holiday* when he finally found *La Mer*...

The sea is exciting, with waves big and small, sand, pebbles (plenty in Brighton) and shells. Comparatively, lakes may seem boring and cold. However, if you think about it, they just have a different personality altogether: still and less noisy.

Like mountains, certain lakes have left a lasting impression in my mind, whether it's because of the colour, the size, the surroundings, the view of or from them, or simply the biases of my personal experience.

1. Big Almaty Lake, Almaty, Kazakhstan
Central Asia

We hired a white four-wheel drive that arrived promptly two hours after we asked for it. The good thing about holidays is that you have an extra layer of patience, compared to a typical day at home or work.

The lake is a three-hour drive from the city centre. I was expecting it to be another potential disappointment, as the photos on Google are often quite flattering and ambitious. However, my cynicism was pushed aside, as we drove closer to the lake. I hadn't seen anything like it before.

A milky-green lake in the middle of mountains south of Almaty. This police-patrolled little gem is the offspring of a couple of earthquakes and global warming, and has an altitude of over 2500m. I was told that the colour would change by season.

2. **Lake Titicaca, Uros Islands, Peru**
   South America

Recruited by our original tour guide, the local tour guide sang 'My Heart Will Go On' on repeat to fill the awkward silence on the boat full of uncomfortable tourists, from Puno to Uros.

It seemed like a long boat ride, but we eventually reached the main island.

Titicaca is the largest lake in South America and is over 3,800m above sea level, shared by Bolivia and Peru. We indulged in fresh fish and chatted to some of the indigenous families who live on one of the 40-odd floating islands made with a bit of DIY, some teamwork, and a lot of reed.

The grandness of the lake, the colourfully-dressed, adorable kids and the unique method of island-construction were just a few of the things to admire.

3. **Iskanderkul, Tajikistan**
   Central Asia

Another one from Central Asia, but it's the best USD 30 I've ever spent on a visa. As our visit took place in July, Tajikistan was generally a scorching, dry nation, but the outskirts were the total opposite.

Sparse villages with friendly Tajiks surrounded the lake, making it a homely, scenic pit-stop for travellers, especially after a long, dusty journey from Dushanbe, in an old saloon car fit for a museum.

Having arrived, I took a local motorboat to make a round trip of this triangular lake. On this occasion, I travelled alone, next to a man who was asking me why I was by myself, and a couple who were being photographed for what I think (and hope) was a swimsuit advert.

The lake itself is just over 2100m above sea level and a bonus view for those trekking the Gissar Range or Fann mountains. The best views are in the morning when it perfectly mirrors the outlines of the mountain tops.

4. Loch Ness & Loch Lomond, Scotland
Europe

I won't forget Loch Ness, not because of the stories about the 'monster', but the drive along the snake-like A82 road beside the waters, leading up to Loch Ness from Loch Lomond.

If you ever read the comic *Tintin* by the Belgian author Hergé, you may also recognise the name of Captain Haddock's Scottish Whisky: Loch Lomond (*Tintin in Picaros*).

Found somewhere between the Scottish Highlands and Lowlands, these lakes are the largest in Britain. Surrounded by villages with stone cottages, friendly locals and *haggis*, those who like trekking can explore Ben Lomond to get the best views of the loch.

5. Lake Lucerne, Switzerland
Central Europe

My parents love Switzerland and so did Bollywood movie directors in the 90s. Growing up, I had built an image of Switzerland as the most beautiful country in the world. We could argue that it is, with no shortage of mountains and lakes.

Lake Lucerne, one of the bigger lakes in Switzerland, is quite a good start for a visit. The best views of the lake are probably from Mount Pilatus or somewhere up on a hill like Chateau Gutsch.

If you're on a budget, simply walk alongside the lake, through the parks where the local Swiss residents go for runs and walks.

6. Lake Victoria, Kenya/Uganda/Tanzania
Africa

Of course, I was going to mention an African lake in this section. I wouldn't say this is the most beautiful lake if you stare into it (it's quite brown), but it's the largest in Africa. It's a unique and special lake as it is a shared baby of three countries, two rivers and the Equator.

Pollution from nearby cities has taken some of its colour and clarity away, but it is still a grand body of water, keeping East Africa hydrated.

There are other lakes that I'd like to pay a visit to during this lifetime, including those below. With my new found trust in Google's images, my internet research showed the following lakes to be the most stunning:

- Lake Baikal, Russia
- Moraine Lake and Peyto Lake, Canada
- Dead Sea, Jordan/Israel
- Tso Moriri, India

Wildlife

According to the WWF (worldwife.org/species), I am now aware that many of the species of wildlife that features in my nephew's 'ABC' alphabet book are now classified as 'endangered' or 'vulnerable'. This makes me wonder how many of them he will actually see as an adult.

'E' for Elephant.
'J' for Jaguar.
'O' for Orangutan.
'P' for Polar Bear.
'R' for Rhino.
'T' for Tiger.
'W' for Whale.

Human existence has obviously tampered with the balance of other living things on the planet, whether it's from carbon emissions, poaching, pollution, plastic production and consumption, and other things posing greater risk to these creatures.

There have been many attempts to help save these threatened species whether it be through fundraising, volunteering or simply changing our daily choices and habits. With all the efforts to protect these species, during my lifetime, I hope that I will be able to see as many of them as possible.

I have unknowingly been on elephant rides in Thailand, where they used a metal hook to make them move. Tourists have even visited the Tiger Temple in Bangkok, Thailand, which is known to have sedated cubs. You can also find very calm and unresponsive lions in some places, such as South Africa, to name a few.

Many of us love the thrill of interacting with these wild animals, but sometimes we forget to think about whether the animals have been compromised to achieve that one *Facebook* photo. I am as guilty as others, but it's something I try to be mindful of now. For instance, rather than visit a zoo where animals are in confined spaces, I would always encourage you to opt for a wildlife safari in a nature reserve, where animals are living in their natural habitat.

For those interested in photography, *culturetrip.com* recommends 10 places where you can gain the best face-to-face shots of our fellow living creatures:

1. Orangutans, Borneo
2. Wildebeests, South Africa
3. Whales, Greenland and Canada
4. Tigers, India
5. Kangaroos, Australia
6. Giant Tortoises, Galapagos Islands
7. Penguins, Antarctica
8. Polar bears, Norwegian Arctic
9. Jaguar, Peru
10. Elephants, Botswana

Article: Botswana
Excerpt from srtravels.co.uk

We hopped on our big tourist bus, which took us through the border from Zimbabwe to Botswana. As the immigration office had run out of forms, we didn't have to fill any in.

While driving, we saw a couple of elephants at the side of the road, including one casually grazing on some leaves and giving itself a little back scratch on a less fortunate tree.

Having arrived at our campsite in Chobe, we set up our tents. The discovery of the rather treacherous ants was very unpleasant but was to be expected – after all we were camping in a National Park. We decided to eat all of our biscuits, before the ants did.

Sunset Cruise

In the afternoon, we set off for a sunset cruise on a large boat, paying around USD 50. I'm not sure how much I would recommend this, but we did see crocodiles swimming, and elephants having a little bath in the hot weather.

The sunset was gorgeous, and the champagne offered by one of our travel buddies for their birthday made it even more enjoyable. A nice way to end our first day in Botswana.

Chobe National Park

I woke up early for the overland safari drive in Chobe National Park and taking one look at the dark sky and windy weather, I realised pretty quickly that I would need a jumper or long sleeve shirt.

I climbed onto the less crowded safari truck and actually loved it. What an experience it was; seeing an entire elephant family from a few metres distance, a lioness, hyenas, impalas, a jackal, warthog, mongooses and a wide variety of birds that some of my companions took more interest in than I did. Unfortunately, we didn't see any zebras or giraffes.

Botswana flag

We were told that the Botswana flag features black and white to symbolise the national animal: the zebra. It also signifies the unity between the different races in the country who now live in harmony. The blue represents the bodies of water that are home to many different types of wildlife, including the Okavango Delta and several rivers across the country.

Gweta

After seven hours on the bus, including a pit stop to have our shoes treated for Foot-and-mouth disease (FMD), we arrived at the beautiful baobab island of Gweta.

Gweta is a small village around 200km away from the city of Maun. It was named after the sounds made by the bullfrogs who surface from under the ground when they would like to mate.

The baobab trees in the village are quite wide, to say the least. Apparently, one of them, called the 'Chapman's Baobab' had a 25-metre circumference. However, it sadly collapsed in 2016.

Maun

On the way to Maun, we stopped at a shopping area with a couple of supermarkets, Forex Bureaus and a Wimpy. The shops were basic, but I managed to buy a USD 5 hat for the Okavango Delta. I paid using my debit card, instead of Pulas, the local currency.

Mishaps

After dinner, I thought I'd have a relaxing shower as we were staying at one of the nicer campsites.

However, three things happened, in the following order:

1. There was a wasp in my shower.
2. There was a power cut.
3. I realised that I left my towel in the tent.

Fortunately, I recovered from these issues quickly; the lights came on, my friend found my towel and the wasp disappeared.

Okavango Delta

At 7am we got on two large open trucks, and were driven through sand and thorny bushes to the Okavango Delta. We had not taken any notice about the warnings regarding the risk of inheriting 'African tattoos' from the thorny branches that frequently brushed through the sides of the trucks (and, sometimes, our faces). Thankfully, no permanent damage done.

We reached the small port where long fibre-glass canoes, called 'mokoros', were lying around. Each mokoro carried two people, our daypacks and our five litre water bottles – our supply kit for the island where we were staying overnight.

The 'polers' who navigate the mokoros use a big wooden stick to push them through the shallow waters of the delta. They had pretty cool names, like 'Mr K', 'Flamingo', and 'Mr Bombastic'.

The weather was scorching hot, but the mokoro-ride was pleasant. We were manoeuvred through the delta towards our campsite. On this part of the trip, we saw elephants and giraffes at a distance and even some hippos, although they stayed dipped under water to cool down due to their skin being sensitive to the sun.

Nature and wildlife

Some of us decided to go for a swim in the delta. This was the closest we would get to having a bath – we felt so dirty. The polers took us on our designated mokoros to a clean part of the delta where around ten of us went for a dip while the guys looked out for any uninvited hippos.

Our journey here ended when a leech attached itself to my friend's back. It didn't take long for the rest of us to decide that it was a good time to return to our tents.

We walked around the delta later in the afternoon, intentionally wearing clothes that would camouflage us better from the wildlife, for safety purposes.

We saw giraffes, zebras, wildebeest and a beautiful sunset before heading back on our mokoros to the campsite.

Must haves:

- ☐ Good sunglasses
- ☐ Sun hat
- ☐ Insect repellent
- ☐ Hydration salts
- ☐ Water

Ghanzi

As soon as we reached Ghanzi, the capital of the Kalahari desert, we attended a 'meet and greet' with some of the local tribal bush men and women. Accompanied by a translator, the aim was to see how they live in the desert.

What I learnt from them was that they were excellent improvisers:

1. Ostrich egg shell = Water bottle
2. Animal skin = Clothes
3. Plants = Contraceptive, soap and even laxative

Water

I looked into my plastic bowl of lukewarm water on the third day of our trek on Mount Kilimanjaro. I started to calculate how much I could achieve from this much water:

- ☐ Brushing my teeth
- ☐ Washing my face
- ☐ Anything else as a bonus

In that moment, I remembered the countless mornings at home when I'd left the tap running, as I brushed my teeth.

I often think about water during my travels. When I'm in a foreign country in hot weather and I haven't found a single shop to buy drinking water; when I'm trying to ration my water supply in my Camelbak for a whole day of trekking; when I am using baby wipes as I haven't had access to a shower when camping. These moments have made me appreciate water a lot more.

Did you know...

US: Many locals in Newark have had to queue for hours and rely on government supplied bottled water, in recent years. The ageing pipes, some over 100 years old, corrode and the lead metal in the pipes separates and seeps into the fresh water supply. Lead being poisonous, and potentially damaging to our central nervous systems.

India: The country faces water scarcity issues caused by the rapid growth in urbanisation. There is a high dependence on groundwater for the irrigation of its agriculture-heavy economy.

World: 785 million people in the world do not have access to clean water in close proximity to their home. The charity organisation, *Water Aid*, revealed that this means that it can be a challenge to gain water to do simple tasks, like drink or for the toilets.

Architecture

The buildings surrounding us, and those we see when travelling, have all been developed during the course of history. Influences from climate, architectural fashion, dominant political and social groups, and many other factors are also evident.

There are so many different forms of architecture; we could spend our entire lives looking at buildings and still find another unfamiliar style, that's still fascinating.

From Khmer carvings (Angkor Wat, Cambodia), Islamic domes (Hagia Sophia, Turkey), Incan estates (Machu Picchu, Peru) to Baroque and Colonial structures (Gothic quarter, Barcelona), there is a limitless world of architectural styles to explore.

Temples, mosques or mausoleums, churches, chapels or cathedrals were built for purpose across the world. In most cases, they remain places to seek refuge, practise religion and faith or for tourists to just appreciate the beauty of their construction.

Meanwhile the UN estimates that by 2050 there will be 6.7 billion people living in the world's cities – 75 percent of the global population (Navigant Research, 2019).

This asks for a continuous demand for more skyscrapers, expanding cities and more innovative modern architecture.

Article: Holy-days
Excerpt from srtravels.co.uk

Angkor Wat
Siem Reap, Cambodia

This is the largest and most impressive temple I've been to. Despite the wake-up call at 3am, it was the most amazing experience from my travels. We dressed in conservative clothes, covering our legs and arms, and hopped on a minibus to get to Angkor Wat ('Wat' means temple).

The sunrise and the reflection of the temple in the still waters, made the lack of sleep totally worth it, even with a hangover.

On a different note, I attract salespeople; even if they're children. There are plenty of them at Angkor Wat. In particular, one annoying little boy attempted to sell me everything from magnets, bracelets, those elephant-print trousers (you know the ones I'm talking about) and postcards. When I politely dismissed the many offers, I was even called a 'bad person'. Ouch.

Anyway, once we'd escaped the little pests, the day got hotter. In over thirty-degrees heat, we walked up far too many steps to reach the top of the temple.

The tour guide rambled on for ages, but we learnt how this Hindu temple in Cambodia, with all the carvings of 'God-Kings' and 'Apsaras' (beautiful Goddesses), was built by over 300,000 labourers and 6000 elephants, using 'holy' sandstone from the Phnom Kulen mountain, transported by rafts over the river*.... and we thought our jobs were tough.

No wonder it took forty years to build.

Source: Lonely Planet, 2019

Sagrada Familia
Barcelona, Spain

This one is still going and is still incomplete. An expected completion date will be in 2026.

Before my first visit to Spain, everyone who'd ever been to Barcelona wouldn't stop talking about [Antoni] Gaudí, the architect who died in 1926.

One of his largest projects, the construction of Sagrada Familia, commenced in the 1880s. This Basilica, also known as the Church of the Holy Family, is the largest Roman Catholic church in the world.

St Paul's Cathedral
London, England

I used to work a few minutes' walk away from this beautiful cathedral. Quite often I used to take the longer route from the station to work, just so that I could go past St Paul's just to say hi.

The developments in the City of London hasn't hidden the cathedral's beauty. No matter from which angle you look at it, St. Paul's remains perfect. Its dome gives the cityscape more charm, sat amongst all the modern and angular office blocks and skyscrapers.

You can look at St Paul's from the terrace of One New Change, a well-known shopping centre, layered with a lot of glass and prism shapes. Such a modern structure is in sharp contrast to the cathedral.

Alternatively, to enjoy panoramic views of the city, step onto the Millennium Bridge or Bankside across the River Thames. The tradition of St Paul's stands out as a clear anomaly amongst the modern buildings.

The cathedral dates back to the 17th century and was one of

the biggest rebuilding projects after the Great Fire of London in 1666. Make sure you check out the Whispering Gallery when you visit. Pretty awesome.

St Peter's Basilica
Vatican City, Italy

Whilst we were hoping to bump into the Pope, that just didn't happen; he must have been busy.

You need almost half a day to see the Vatican City, the smallest 'country' in the world. By making the very wise decision to use the online booking system to purchase entrance tickets for the Vatican Museum, we managed to skip the queues.

The conservative dress code applies, and I was given a very unattractive, disposable poncho to cover my shoulders.

The inside and outside of the basilica are stunning and the museum was the most impressive I have seen.

The only problem was the number of tourists. July is a very busy month; it felt like I was back into my morning commute in London. Apart from those tiny observations, St. Peter's Basilica is a must for all bucket lists.

Ulugh Beg Madrasah, Registan
Samarkand, Uzbekistan

As one of the three Madrasahs in Registan, a public square in the city of Samarkand, this place made me happy for three reasons:

1. It kept me cool from the ridiculous heat outside.
2. The insides were decorated with detailed gold-leaf designs.
3. The outside was decorated with millions of small ceramic tiles (mostly blue and white).

The Hungry Traveller

In a country that has been ruled by Persians, Greeks, Turks, Mongols, Chinese and Russians, the old city of Samarkand is still famous, mainly because of the Registan, previously occupied by bustling markets and caravanserai (roadside inns).

Did you know...

There are around 4,300 religions around the world.

Almost 75 percent of the world's population practises one of these five religions:

1. Buddhism
2. Christianity
3. Hinduism
4. Islam
5. Judaism

Source: Adherents, an independent, non-religiously affiliated organisation that monitors the number and size of the world's religions.

Article: Vertigology
Excerpt from srtravels.co.uk

Vertigo
ˈvəːtɪgəʊ/ noun
A sensation of whirling and loss of balance, associated particularly with looking down from a great height.

Some people absolutely hate looking down from high rise buildings, vertigo or no vertigo. For me, whether I'm looking up from the bottom of a building, or looking down at the tiny moving cars, I'm in my happy place.

Apart from the impressive skill and architecture, labour and project management involved in constructing each of the buildings, they have become statement pieces for cities all over the world.

Some more well-known than others, here are a number of buildings that I'd recommend visiting, especially for the view from the top.

Eiffel Tower
Paris, France

I know this is like stating the obvious, however, apparently some people think it's ugly. By delving deeper into its history, we learn to admire it a bit more.

The Eiffel Tower has been around for over 130 years, acting as a symbol of Paris for tourists around the world. Built to mark the 100th anniversary of the French Revolution, it's the same height as an 81-storey building, although technically it only has three floors. I've never taken the 704 stairs to the top, but it's equally nice to use the elevator to save time and tick it off your bucket list.

Height: 300m
Floors: 3
Claim to fame: marks the 100th anniversary of the
French Revolution
Since: 1887

The Shard
London, England

As the tallest building in Western Europe, I feel like I should
mention the Shard. I wouldn't say it's my favourite tourist
attraction, but I feel it now has the same symbolic feel to it as
the 'Eiffel Tower for London', i.e. the statement piece for the
London skyline, visible from miles away.

The question must also be asked: what is the reason for
leaving the top of the tower incomplete?

Apparently, it's both a metaphor for a 'constantly evolving
London', as well as allowing any excess heat to rise to the
top, and out to the skies.

Height: 309.6m
Floors: 95
Claim to fame: Western Europe's tallest building
Since: 2013

CN Tower
Toronto, Canada

The CN Tower also offers another unique symbolic
feel, similar to that of the Eiffel Tower. Simply, it's a
communications and observation tower made of concrete.
The added feature of an 'Edge walk' allowing groups of six
to walk hands-free around the tower makes this the world's
highest full circle hands-free walk at 356m above the ground.

If you're squeamish at that thought of 'hanging out', then you could just spend time in the 360-bar. At this very location, we spent long periods of time watching planes taking off and landing at Toronto Island Airport.

Height: 553m
Floors: 144
Claim to fame: it was the world's tallest free-standing structure for over 30 years, until 2007.
Since: 1976

Empire State Building
New York, USA

As a child, the word 'skyscraper' had many connotations but the Empire State Building was the first that would spring to mind. After all, it was the tallest building in the world for almost 40 years.

The museum on the second highest floor is interesting; black and white images of the labourers who worked on the building are clearly presented. Construction of this staggering building took just over one year.

Location at the core of New York City, this trademark skyscraper is open 365 days a year. In fact, it plays around in the night skyline with different colour schemes, whether it's the usual white, or the Stars and Stripes. The building has a unique aura of moodiness.

Height: 443m
Floors: 102
Claim to fame: tallest building in the world for almost 40 years
Since: 1931

Petronas Towers
Kuala Lumpur, Malaysia

These towers are an iconic symbol of Kuala Lumpur. The Petronas Towers were inspired by the fourth Prime Minister of Malaysia, Tun Mahathir Mohamad who had a vision for the country to be a global contender.

It took seven years to build and involved daily transfers of over 500 trucks of material, as well as digging 30 metres below ground level. It's mostly made of concrete but the steel and glass 'look' is intended to reflect the country's Islamic art and religion.

Height: 452m
Floors: 88
Claim to fame: tallest twin towers in the world.
Since: 2001

Did you know...

- In earlier times, the tallest buildings in a town or city were meant to be religious.
- The largest number of skyscrapers were built in 2016 (128 towers over 200m tall).
- As of 2019, Burj Khalifa (Dubai) is the tallest man-made building in the world (830m tall).
- Spain has an M-shaped skyscraper (Intempo) with 47 floors.
- Taiwan's Taipei 101 is the tallest environmentally-friendly building in the world. The lift can take visitors from the 5th to the 89th floor in less than 40 seconds.

Transportation

Walking the streets of London, I see plenty of modern modes of transport: cycles, scooters, motorbikes, cars, vans, buses, trucks.

We also have the infamous London Underground, packed with commuters en route to their place of work.

Many European cities have trams, while Wuppertal in Germany has an electric railway with hanging cars, called the Suspension Railway.

When travelling to different countries, there will be many things that you will see that are unique to that country and culture and are special enough to turn your head.

Cyclo

Walking on the streets of Hanoi, I saw a single seater Cyclo with a driver at the back and passenger seat in front. I hopped on and having been flung from side to side and dodging hundreds of other scooters on the road, I wasn't convinced I would return in one piece. Despite this, it was absolutely fun and, actually, very enjoyable.

Rickshaw

From the 1930s, rickshaws have been an active part of life in a number of countries across South and East Asia, including India, Pakistan, Bangladesh and, later, Indonesia. Even in modern-day London, near tourist spots like Oxford Street, rickshaws have found a new home for locals and tourists. These pedal-powered two-seaters, with a driver in front, are a leisurely mode of transport. Previously in Kolkata, India, instead of a cycle, someone would pull the whole thing and run with their bare feet (think of *The Flintstones*).

Unsurprisingly foot-powered rickshaws were banned for safety reasons and due to the increase of automobiles on the roads.

Tangahs and Horse carts

An upgrade from a cycle-rickshaw, these carts with a horse or two are probably a more exotic and, sometimes, faster mode of transport in places like India, Pakistan and, even, Poland. With wooden wheels, the ride may not be as smooth, but it's still a good experience.

Coco Taxis and Tuktuks

Tuktuks are found in several cities around South and East Asia these days. Essentially, these are three-wheelers which you could call an upgrade from a scooter.

Places with Tuktuks (names may vary): Thailand, India, China, Indonesia, Cambodia, Sri Lanka, Bangladesh and Pakistan.

Coco Taxis are rounder versions of Tuktuks, found in Havana and in Varadero in Cuba,

However, when you hit the water, you will truly experience the ultimate in innovation and improvisation.

Caballitos de Totora

Made of reed, just like the 'land' that the local Peruvian Uros Islanders live on, these have been used by fishermen for the past three millennia. They are named after the way they are straddled like small horses*.

*Caballo = Horse in Spanish.

Mokoros

A type of canoe commonly used in the Okavango Delta, Botswana. They are propelled through the shallow waters by pushing the waterbed with a pole.

Gondola

These carved wooden boats in Venice, Italy are famous with tourists for being super-romantic. They are the perfect way to tour the canals of this beautiful city.

Kettuvallam

These houseboats in Kerala, India navigate the backwaters in a very relaxing way. Wooden planks, coconut fibre, ropes, bamboo poles and palm leaves are used to make the houseboats.

Did you know...

Boat and Rail
In Jules Verne's story *Around the World in Eighty Days* the fictional character Phileas Fogg (theme for Mr & Mrs Fogg's cocktail bars in London) travelled around the world by boat and rail. This actually happened in 1889 when American journalist Nellie Bly performed a circumnavigation i.e. world tour in 72 days using boats and railways.

Bicycle
Another crazy idea was from Alastair Humphreys, a British traveller, who cycled 74,000 km through five continents and 60 countries. It took him four years.

Aeroplane
The average commercial jet liner travels about 550 mph, and the Earth is around 26,000 miles in circumference. Therefore, a plane could circumnavigate the planet in around 40 – 50 hours.

Article: Rush Hour in London, England
Excerpt from srtravels.co.uk

Rush hour
noun
A time during each day when traffic is at its heaviest.

Apart from forcing us to learn more about our anger management, rush hour in any busy city, especially the City of London, can teach us a lot about ourselves.

Rush hour is a total learning curve for anyone taking part; avoiding eye contact, testing your patience, resilience and physical abilities, choosing the right outfits and understanding how to manoeuvre through the city.

1. **Eye contact**

    If I'm on a train or bus or am waiting at a platform and I feel like someone is looking in my direction, the first step is to narrow down the reasons why. For instance:

    *   They are looking past me*
    *   They forgot to look away
    *   They know me
    *   They are crazy
    *   I have something on my face
    *   They like my face
    *   They don't like my face
    *   They are partially sighted
    *   They are cross-eyed
    *   They are creepy

    *Most preferable option

The next step is to understand how to deal with this not-so-comfortable situation. The absolute last option is a risky one; you can stare back at the 'starer' until they hopefully look away, However, this could backfire, unless you're good at staring games.

The following are some tried and tested ideas to keep yourself occupied:

- (Pretend to) sleep
- Read a book or newspaper
- Play Candy Crush
- (Re-)Read your *WhatsApp* messages
- Go through all your photos
- Get some work done
- Unsubscribe from all your junk emails
- Meditate (Calm App is pretty good)
- Read the poster about '*Pregnacare*' on repeat
- Listen to music or watch a movie
- Stare out of the window

2. **Yoga**

There will be times when you'll be surprised at what your body can do when it doesn't have a choice while travelling on a packed train. Even if it's yoga or your usual stretching exercises.

Here are five things worth practising at home prior to rush hour:

- One-leg stands: to avoid stepping on someone's foot, luggage, child or a dog's tail.
- Surf: when you can't hold on to anything on a moving train, you'll need to work on your balancing skills and lower your centre of gravity.
- Neck rotations: for when you have to move your neck to one side to avoid being face to face with a stranger or their armpit.

- Arm stretches: you should be able to twist your arm backwards in order to hold the one pole you can just about reach past another five bodies or avoid skin-to-skin contact in the hotter months of summer.
- *PAŚCIMOTTĀNĀSANA:* a forward sitting bend for when you're lucky enough to get a seat, but unlucky enough to have neighbouring passengers who are large or are selfish enough to take over the armrests.

3. Dress like an onion

I once made the grave mistake of wearing a winter coat, boots, a polo neck thermal, a woolly skirt, hat and gloves on the London Underground's Central Line.

Seemingly, this is the second hottest tube line in London during summer, but even in winter, this line is deceiving. You'll need to have an escape strategy from your very own clothes during any season.

I learnt the hard way that a polo neck top is not easy to get out of in general, and even more so during rush hour, while standing in very close proximity to fellow commuters. Even removing a jumper or jacket grabs far more attention during rush hour than is necessary.

This removal of clothing involves excessive squirming, and what may look like a bad snake-dance, while attempting to keep a straight face and 'playing it cool'.

The solution?

Dress like an onion. Wear several layers of clothes that you can peel off one by one, seamlessly, without touching your neighbouring passenger. Stick to thin layers, unless you fancy looking like Joey from the TV show *Friends* when he put on all of Chandler's clothes.

Remember to have enough space in your bag to carry all the removed layers, especially if you decide to leave the station and re-join the outside world.

4. Slow walkers

I'm not referring to people who are older or less mobile, I'm talking about people who somehow manage to look at their mobile phone, or even more surprisingly read a book while walking down a narrow pathway, oblivious to who or what is behind them.

The good thing about London is that most commuters have learnt to invest in comfortable walking shoes, purely for speed. Invest in a good pair and you, hopefully, won't be one of the slow walkers annoying everyone else. There is always the option to pop the less comfortable shoes into your bag, or leave them at work.

5. Hygiene

When using public transport, apart from real people and much needed entertainment, your best friends need to be the following:

- Hand sanitiser
- A mask (although I haven't picked up the courage to buy or wear one yet).

These could help us prevent suffering the consequences of unwanted pollution.

Whether it's a fellow passenger's poor body odour, bad breath, post-night out alcohol sweats, serial coughing or a sneezing neighbour who thinks it's okay not to cover their mouth or nose, or those who didn't find the time to file their nails... there's plenty of unhygienic practices you might want to avoid while travelling on buses, tubes or trains.

In summary, rush hour may appear impossible to survive on a daily basis, especially when travelling on public transport in London. However, it is possible to prepare for it and hopefully master the art of the 'Commute'.

Carbon Footprint vs. Body Mass Index

The reality is that I am no Phileas Fogg and I can't travel the world by boat or train, especially with twenty-something days of annual leave.

Sometimes, we have to fulfil our personal goals and priorities, while being conscious of the environment and deal with our decision-making in a balanced way.

An increasing number of people are talking about our individual carbon footprint – the amount of greenhouse gases released into the atmosphere by certain types of human activity.

In my mind, I look at an individual's carbon footprint in the same way as we measure our Body Mass Index (BMI). Both are very broad measures, based on our habits and behaviour and the impact it has on the health of our world and our bodies.

Although BMI can be a good general indication of whether you're obese or overweight, it's not always accurate. Whilst high BMI results can trigger an individual to take action to correct it, some people who are classified as overweight from a BMI calculation*, are actually very fit and muscular.

*BMI = Your weight (kg) / Your height (m) x Your height (m)
A healthy BMI is considered to be between 18.5 to 24.9.

Having said that, an awareness of BMI can still be a good place to start for some people.

In the same sense that a high BMI can make us think about whether we could eat less or more healthily and / or change our exercise routines, a carbon footprint calculation could also encourage us to review our lifestyles.

Could we live better and try to minimise the damage our existence does to the wider world?

Every little helps. Maybe.

You can calculate your carbon footprint on *footprint.wwf.org.uk* where it's based on four main categories:

1. Food
2. Travel
3. Home
4. Things

According to WWF (2019), the average carbon footprint per person is 5 tonnes and the UK average is 12.5 tonnes.

Unsurprisingly, my personal carbon footprint was higher than the UK average. When I broke this down further, 70 percent was due to long-haul flights.

However, it appears that the issue is more than just me and my return trips to Dubai (to visit my brother and family).

According to the UNWTO's tourism dashboard (unwto.org), the split between the different modes of transport used by travellers in 2018 were:

- Air: 58 percent
- Road: 37 percent
- Water: 3 percent
- Rail: 2 percent

One way to minimise our air travel could be to visit multiple countries using one return flight. For instance, after our flight from London to Victoria Falls in Zimbabwe, we continued our journey to Botswana and Namibia by road.

There is debate around whether carbon offsetting is as efficient as we like to think. So, it's up to you to decide whether you would like to try to offset your carbon footprint for a very reasonable amount of money.

An example calculation from *co2.myclimate.org* shows that an Economy Class round trip from London to Kolkata via Dubai for one traveller is around 15,500km, which equates to around 2.6 tonnes of carbon emissions.

The cost to offset these emissions is quoted at USD 70. There are several international and sustainable development projects that could be selected for the money to go to. These projects contribute to the UN's Sustainable Development Goals (SDGs).

In effect, as long as research on the authenticity of these companies reveals they are genuine, this is a bit like fundraising for the future of the world.

Whether you're on holiday or not, the next five actions could help lower your carbon footprint:

1. Minimise use of plastic bags, or reuse them.
2. Consider booking fewer long-haul flights.
3. Consume more food from local markets, rather than supermarkets.
4. If you eat meat, reduce the amount.
5. Switch off lights in empty rooms.

City Edit: Kolkata, India
Excerpt from srtravels.co.uk

This city holds deep meaning for me personally. This is the city where my parents met, where my brother was born and where we spent most of our Christmas holidays when I was growing up.

In response to the way many locals referred to their cities, Kolkata's name changed from Calcutta in 2001, along with several other major cities in India. Personally, I thought Calcutta sounded nicer.

Kolkata was India's capital during British Colonial times, between 1773 and 1911. Today, it is known for its grand colonial architecture, art and culture, food, pollution (sadly) and is also known as the City of Joy.

Organised chaos

Despite the chaos of Kolkata, everyone seems to work well within this strange system of no system. The cars, people, rickshaws, cycles and buses might look like they are all going to collide with each other at any point, but they usually don't. I have seen quite a few indifferent old people casually walk in front of cars to cross the road, without a hint of being afraid. The vehicle drivers do not seem to care about the pedestrian crossings either. So, to get to the other side of the road, unless you fancy standing for a long time, you will need to brave it.

Languages

The main spoken language is Bengali. This is the same language, in its purest form, as the national language of Bangladesh. However, over the years, the dialects in Bangladesh have evolved to sound completely different. It is one of 22 languages spoken in India. Other languages spoken include Nepali, Oriya and Hindi, as well as some that I have never heard of.

History and Landmarks

Before New Delhi, Calcutta was the capital of India and still has an obvious sense of the British colonial times. The Victoria Memorial, built in memory of Queen Victoria, is one of the main landmarks. Resembling the regal Taj Mahal, it is surrounded by serene gardens, students reading under trees, lovers chilling by the ponds, and a line of horse carriages (Tangas) waiting outside the gates to charge tourists extortionate amounts of money (by local standards) for a ten-minute round trip.

Note: negotiation is common in Kolkata. Depending on how foreign you look, you are more likely to be overcharged. However, even after being overcharged, it's still cheap.

Food

You can pick and choose between all the street food stalls, including *kathi rolls* and *phuchka* (hollow crispy balls of flour, stuffed with spicy potato, dipped into minty water and served really, really quickly). Customers circle around the *phuchka* seller, the *phuchka* themselves are served one at a time on disposable, environmentally friendly mini bowls made from dry leaves. Sometimes, I may not have finished one before being served the next, and they keep serving until you hold your hand up and /or tell them to stop.

In terms of food in general, as long as you are careful where you eat, I personally think Kolkata has some of the best varieties of flavoursome food: from chicken-egg rolls (*kathi rolls*), to *biriyani* to *Indo-Chinese* food and a huge variety of Bengali *mishti* (sweets).

Shopping

Kolkata feels like a massive market. You can purchase pretty much anything: food, jewellery, accessories, clothes, shoes, kitchenware, furniture, paintings, miniature models of Hindu Gods, clocks or electrical items. Almost all of these things are sold on the streets of the city on small stalls.

There are obviously bigger shops and quite a few shopping centres with the international and high-quality brands, but the real fun is haggling with the street vendors.

Transport

- Auto-rickshaw (3-wheelers)
- Rickshaw (cycle or 'Tanga')
- Metro (underground)
- Yellow taxi (do it for the old-school bumpy ride experience!)
- Uber or Ola (you can pay with cash)
- Walk

The environment

One of the main problems in the city is pollution. More recently, Kolkata is just behind megacities Chengdu, Delhi, London and New York in terms of reducing carbon emissions. The city is pioneering greener commutes across the city involving more electric buses and ferries, making it fifth on a list of places that are reducing their annual emissions (Source: World Economic Forum; weforum.org/agenda/2019).

Did you know...

Approximately 7,111 languages are spoken around the world today, while only 23 languages account for more than half the world's population.

Source: Ethnologue: a research centre for language intelligence.

Top 10 most spoken languages in the world:

1. Mandarin Chinese
2. Spanish
3. English
4. Hindi
5. Arabic
6. Bengali
7. Portuguese
8. Russian
9. Japanese
10. Lahnda (Western Punjabi)

Source: Babbel.com

Part Two: Explore Food

Foodie
/ˈfuːdi/ noun

A person with a particular interest in food; a gourmet.

Local Cuisines

During the course of my travels, I always bring back two specific things from every place I visit:

1. Cheap souvenirs (as discussed already)
2. Memories linked to the local cuisine

My adventurous taste buds have gotten my stomach into trouble on several occasions, but that hasn't stopped me from bouncing back to try the next new dish I set my eyes (and nose) on.

Obviously, I try to make informed choices of where to eat. I benchmark my decision by looking at the hustle and bustle of the restaurant or food stall, popularity, online ratings, general hygiene, stickiness of the floors, tables, menus etc.

Although, when I'm hungry I tend to go common-sense-blind until I eat. I'm pretty sure I've almost lost a few friends because of my *hanger* (hunger + anger).

I've been fortunate enough to savour a vast array of foods from around the world. Interestingly, I've increasingly noticed that there are similarities in the gastronomy from places that are not necessarily within close geographical proximity.

For instance:

> Polish or Czech *dumplings* vs. Pan-Asian *momos;*
> German *schnitzel* vs. French *escalope;*
> Hungarian *goulash* vs. Moroccan *tagine;*
> Dutch *bitterballen* vs. Finnish *lihapullat;*
> British *Scotch egg* vs. Indian *nargis kofte.*

Flavours, recipes, ingredients and nutrition can speak volumes about the history of a country, from the tastes of the inhabitants to the civilisations they traded with.

In this section, we'll explore food through hand-picked food and drink from some of the countries I've been to, with supporting recipes.

Although my culinary skills are close to basic, I believe many of these recipes are beginner-friendly.

A lot of the dishes I have featured include meat, fish, eggs and alcohol. As the world is increasingly vegan, health-conscious and ethical I've tried to suggest alternative ingredients for most recipes, to make them more relevant for most of us. I hope.

Bon Appétit…

… and you could choose to toast with:

1. Cheers: English
2. Gān bēi: Chinese (Mandarin)
3. Lechyd da ('Yeh-ki-dah'): Welsh
4. Prost: German
5. Proost: Dutch
6. Salute (or Cin Cin): Italian
7. Salud: Spanish
8. Santé: French
9. Saúde: Portuguese
10. Skål ('Skawl'): Swedish
11. Sláint ('Slawn-cha'): Irish Gaelic
12. ΥΓΕΙΑ ('Yamas'): Greek
13. Na zdrowie: Polish

Key:

 = Savoury

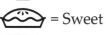 = Sweet

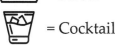 = Cocktail

Global Menu

Item	Country	Continent	Type	Dietary notes
Lok Lak	Cambodia	Asia	Savoury	Contains meat
Qurutob	Tajikistan	Asia	Savoury	Vegetarian option
Pad Thai	Thailand	Asia	Savoury	Vegetarian option
Pupusa	El Salvador	Americas	Savoury	Vegetarian option
Caipirinha	Brazil	Americas	Cocktail	Contains alcohol
Pisco Sour	Peru	Americas	Cocktail	Contains alcohol
Sukuma Wiki	Kenya	Africa	Savoury	Vegetarian option
Matoke	Uganda	Africa	Savoury	Vegetarian option
Tagine	Morocco	Africa	Savoury	Vegetarian option
Scotch Egg	UK	Europe	Savoury	Contains eggs
Pastéis de Nata	Portugal	Europe	Sweet	Contains eggs
Guinness Cake	Ireland	Europe	Sweet	Contains eggs

Taste of Asia

Lok Lak (or *Loc Lac*)

Cambodia

A perfectly balanced meal.

If you're in Cambodia, the next best thing after watching the sunrise at Angkor Wat, is to have a *lok lak*.

When travelling, I tend to avoid having salads. The main reason is for fear that they haven't been washed or are a bit 'old'. Despite this, I had to pinch some of the fresh green salad underneath the beef, including cucumbers and rings of raw onions. It comes with some extra magical sauce and, sometimes, a fried egg and / or rice.

This dish simply gets better and better.

> **Prep time:** 15 mins (plus 1 hour to marinate the meat)
> **Cook time:** 30 mins
> **Serves:** 4
> **Ingredients:**
>
> **For the marinade:**
> - ☐ 3 tbsp tomato sauce
> - ☐ 3 tbsp soy sauce
> - ☐ 3 cloves garlic, chopped
> - ☐ ¼ tsp salt
> - ☐ 5 tbsp fish sauce
> - ☐ ¼ tsp *Kampot* pepper
> - ☐ 2 tbsp sugar
> - ☐ 3 tbsp vegetable oil
> - ☐ 1 tsp chicken broth powder
> - ☐ 2 tsp potato starch (or corn starch)
> - ☐ 3 tsp paprika

For the Sauce:
- ☐ Juice of 5 limes
- ☐ 3 tbsp cold water
- ☐ ¼ tsp salt
- ☐ 2 cloves garlic, chopped
- ☐ 2 tsp sugar
- ☐ 1 tbsp fish sauce
- ☐ 2 tbsp vegetable oil
- ☐ ½ tsp pepper

For Everything else:
- 1.5 lbs of lamb or beef steak, sliced or cubed
- A few lettuce leaves
- 2 tomatoes, sliced
- Steamed white rice

Method:
- ☐ Mix all the marinade ingredients in a salad bowl, add the meat and stir well.
- ☐ Marinate the meat for 1 hour in the refrigerator.
- ☐ Heat the vegetable oil in a wok and add the meat, mix well and sauté for 5 to 10 mins.
- ☐ In a bowl, stir all the ingredients of the *lok lak* sauce.
- ☐ Prepare large plates.
- ☐ On each plate, place a bed of lettuce leaves and a few slices of tomato.
- ☐ Place the meat on the lettuce and tomatoes.
- ☐ Serve with steamed white rice.
- ☐ Place a small bowl of *lok lak* sauce on the side or the centre of each plate.

Source: 196flavors.com

Qurutob

Tajikistan

A personal reason for my happiness in this Central Asian country can be attributed to my hosts at a homestay, a mother and two daughters. When preparing one of their main national dishes, *qurutob* in their small kitchen, they noticed my boredom and invited me to chop the onions.

During my visit, I was staying at their village house in the area around Iskanderkul, surrounded by mountains and streams connecting the glorious triangular lake.

Even though they spoke no English and I spoke no Russian or Tajik, I gathered that:

- They were fond of India (which they referred to as *Hindustan*).
- If I lived there, I would have been married by the age of 22.
- My onion-chopping skills weren't good enough as they re-chopped the ones I did.

Qurutob was my first solid meal. During my time with them, they had served a lot of beef broth soup for most meals; to be fair, it's probably more cost-effective. As soon as the *Qurutob* cooled down, I was the first to taste one, just like I do when my mother cooks.

For a brief moment, I felt like I was at home.

Prep time: 15 mins
Cook time: 30 mins
Serves: 4

Ingredients:
- ☐ 4 frozen flatbreads
- ☐ 500 ml Greek yogurt
- ☐ ½ cup water
- ☐ 2 tsp salt
- ☐ 3 tomatoes, diced
- ☐ 2 onions, chopped
- ☐ 2 spring onions, thinly sliced
- ☐ ½ bunch coriander, chopped
- ☐ Vegetable oil

Method:
1. Heat the frozen flatbreads on a flat pan until golden brown.
2. Once these cool down, cut them into small pieces.
3. Heat the Greek yogurt and water in a saucepan over medium heat. Add salt.
4. Stir regularly for 30 mins.
5. The result should yield about ⅔ of the initial weight of yogurt, e.g. 400 ml.
6. Sauté onion in a skillet in hot oil until translucent, about 8 mins.
7. Meanwhile, place small pieces of the bread in a large bowl (traditionally a large wooden dish) and top the bread pieces with yogurt.
8. Pour the onion with the hot oil on top of that.
9. Top with spring onions, tomatoes and coriander.
10. Serve immediately.

Source: 196flavors.com for the qurutob (note that the frozen flatbread suggestion is my own, because life is too short).

Pad Thai

Thailand

I had my first *Pad Thai* in Chiang Mai, Thailand. This began my *Pad Thai* obsession.

The dish is basically stir-fried rice noodles and is the national dish of Thailand. It was introduced in the 1930s to create its own identity and is completely separate from the Chinese version. According to *CNN Go* in 2011, it was even listed as one of the world's most delicious foods.

The recipe below is quick and easy, which is why lazy people like me like it even more.

Prep time: 10 mins
Cook time: 5 mins
Serves: 4

Ingredients:

For the *pad thai*:
- ☐ 4 ounces rice noodles
- ☐ 1 courgette
- ☐ 1 red pepper
- ☐ Half an onion
- ☐ 2 carrots
- ☐ 2 tbsp oil
- ☐ 1 egg, beaten
- ☐ ½ cup peanuts, chopped
- ☐ ½ cup fresh herbs like coriander and basil

For the sauce:
- ☐ 3 tbsp fish sauce or vegan fish sauce
- ☐ 3 tbsp brown sugar
- ☐ 3 tbsp chicken or vegetable broth
- ☐ 2 tbsp white vinegar
- ☐ 1 tbsp soy sauce
- ☐ 1 tsp chilli paste

Method:
1. Place the uncooked noodles in a bowl of cold water to soak.
2. Cut the courgette, carrots, red pepper, and onion into noodle-like shapes.
3. Shake up the sauce ingredients in a jar.
4. Heat a tbsp of oil over medium high heat.
5. Add the vegetables; stir fry for 2-3 mins or until tender-crisp. Be careful not to overcook as they'll get soggy and heavy. Transfer to a dish and set aside.
6. Add another tbsp of oil to the pan.
7. Drain the noodles and add them to the hot pan and stir fry for a minute.
8. Add the sauce and stir fry for another minute or two, until the sauce is starting to thicken and stick to the noodles.
9. Push the noodles aside to make a little room for the egg. Pour the beaten egg into the pan and let it sit for approximately 30 seconds.
10. Toss everything around and let the egg mixture stick to the noodles and everything will start to get sticky.
11. Add in the vegetables, toss together, and remove from heat.
12. Stir in the peanuts and herbs and serve immediately.

Source: Pinchofyum.com

Taste of Americas

Pupusa

El Salvador

Just imagine yourself walking down the hilly streets of Ataco, El Salvador with a *pupusa* in one hand and camera in the other, admiring the views of the green hills…

Apart from the beautiful hand-painted and colourful murals on every wall, *pupusas* became my personal favourite within 24 hours of being there.

Don't make the mistake of going by their funny name.

These delicious and versatile little round stuffed flatbreads are served hot and made by homely women on the corners of the streets in Ataco. Each *pupusa* costs around 50 cents. Needless to say, we had at least a couple. Although they are small, due to the corn flour, they are quite filling and delicious.

There is a choice of stuffings vegetarian, non-vegetarian, or both.

Prep time: 30 mins
Cooking time: 5 mins
Serves: 5 (25 *pupusas*)

Ingredients:

For the *pupusas:*
- ☐ 4 cups of maize flour
- ☐ 3 ½–4 cups warm water
- ☐ ½ tsp salt
- ☐ 2 tbsp butter, softened (optional)

For the filling:
- ☐ 1 can refried beans
- ☐ 2 cups shredded mozzarella
- ☐ 1 cup of minced meat or chicken for a non-vegetarian option

Method:
1. Add maize flour and salt to a large mixing bowl.
2. Add the warm water, little by little, mixing the dough with your hand.

   Note: You may not need all of the water. You want the maize flour to be the consistency of a soft play dough. If the dough is too wet, mix in some more maize flour. If it's too dry, add a little more water.

3. Mix in the melted butter
4. Scoop the dough into golf-ball-size portions.

   Note: You can scoop all of the dough into balls before continuing, or make one pupusa at a time. Be sure to keep the dough covered with a damp cloth as you work, to keep it from drying out.

5. Use the palms of your hands to pat the dough into a disc, about 4 inches in diameter.
6. Take half a tbsp of the beans and place in the centre of the dough circle, followed by a pinch of shredded cheese.
   For the non-vegetarian option, lightly stir-fry the mincemeat or chicken and add a tbsp. of it in the centre as well.
7. Gently bring the edges of the dough up and around the filling, pinching it closed into a ball.
8. Gently pat the dough between your palms to form it into a disc again.
9. Heat a large ungreased pan over medium heat.

10. Place the *pupusas* on the hot pan and cook for about 2-4 mins on each side.

   Note: You will know the pupusas are ready to flip when the edges are set and the bottom is lightly golden.

11. Serve hot.

Source: Tastesbetterfromscratch.com

Caipirinha

Brazil

My travels to Brazil seemed like every night, afternoon or morning was a party. To hold onto these memories, I ordered a few bottles of *cachaça* as soon as I returned from Brazil. *Cachaça* is a spirit made from sugar cane juice itself, giving it a grassy taste, and differentiating it from similar spirits like rum.

Caipirinhas are the staple drink in Brazil and they're very easy to make, with only four ingredients.

Prep time: 5 mins
Mixing time: 5 mins
Serves: 1

Ingredients:
- ☐ ½ lime
- ☐ 1 tbsp brown sugar
- ☐ 50ml of *cachaça*
- ☐ Crushed ice

Method:
1. Cut one green lime into wedges so that they look like little triangles and put them into a nice (whisky) glass.
2. Add a tbsp of brown sugar.
3. Pour the *cachaça* into the glass.
4. Use a pestle to crush the lime in the glass.
5. Add crushed ice so that as the ice melts, it dilutes the drink.
6. Enjoy (slowly).

Source: Thewanderlustkitchen.com

Pisco Sour

Peru

This is the first time I was comfortable with drinking raw egg white in my drink.

We relaxed by a pool next to the Huacachina Oasis, Peru, not too far from Lima, while sipping on our *pisco sours*. Before I knew it, I was on my third, foregoing the option to go sandboarding near the oasis.

Pisco is a type of brandy produced in Peru and Chile, made from fermented grape juice and was developed during the countries' Spanish colonial times.

I have yet to make one myself, but there are so many bars in London that make it perfectly so, I haven't had the need to... yet.

Prep time: 10 mins
Mixing time: 5 mins
Serves: 1

Ingredients:
- ☐ 60 ml pisco
- ☐ 30 ml simple syrup
- ☐ 30 ml fresh egg white
- ☐ 30 ml lime juice
- ☐ 6 drops of Angostura bitters

Method:
1. Add all ingredients into a shaker with ice and shake vigorously.
2. Strain into a glass over fresh ice.
3. Garnish with 3 drops of the bitters.
4. Using a straw, swirl the bitters into a simple design.

Source: Liquor.com

Taste of Africa

Sukuma Wiki

Kenya

I grew up in Kenya sharing this dish with (or stealing from) the lady who was our household help. *Sukuma wiki* is a very popular dish in many parts of East Africa, including Kenya. In the local language of Swahili, it means to 'stretch the week'. It is often paired with *ugali* – cornmeal.

Prep time: 10 mins
Cook time: 15 mins
Serves: 3 – 4

Ingredients:
- ☐ 1 kale bunch or collard greens
- ☐ 3 medium tomatoes, diced
- ☐ 1-2 tsp minced garlic
- ☐ 1 large white onion
- ☐ 2 or more tbsp vegetable oil
- ☐ 1 tbsp smoked paprika
- ☐ ½ tsp coriander
- ☐ ½ tsp curry or turmeric spice
- ☐ ½ tsp cayenne pepper or more
- ☐ ½ juiced lemon (about 1 tbsp)
- ☐ 1 tbsp vegetable stock
- ☐ 1-2 cups beef/chicken mince for a non-vegetarian option

Method:

1. Add oil, onions, and garlic to a pan and sauté for two mins, stirring constantly.
2. Add the tomatoes, curry, coriander and paprika, and continue stirring for another two mins.
3. Add vegetable stock (and the mince if appropriate) and keep stirring.
4. After five mins, add the chopped kale / collards, cayenne pepper, lemon juice and cook for another 10 mins maximum.
5. Once cooked, serve with *ugali*.

Source: Africanbites.com

Matoke

Uganda

Matoke is basically plantains, which are the staple crop in Uganda. It is filling, nutritious and can, again, be combined with meat if preferred.

Having lived in the capital city, Kampala for six years, we had plenty of *matoke* in our school lunches, to keep us youngsters strong and healthy.

Our family's weekly shop involved a trip to *Nakasero Market,* where local vendors bring in the food that is produced from the farmland.

The red soil in Uganda, the 'Pearl of Africa' is one of the most fertile in the world. It is no accident that the produce here is so healthy and tasty.

> **Prep time:** 10 mins
> **Cook time:** 30 mins
> **Serves:** 4 - 6
>
> **Ingredients:**
> - ☐ 8–10 plantains
> - ☐ 1 lemon, juice of (optional)
> - ☐ Oil (for frying)
> - ☐ 1 onion, chopped
> - ☐ 2–3 tomatoes, chopped (or canned whole tomatoes, drained)
> - ☐ 1 green bell pepper, chopped
> - ☐ 3–4 garlic cloves, crushed
> - ☐ 1 chilli pepper, chopped (optional)

Method:
1. Peel the plantains and cut them into cubes, sprinkle with lemon juice, and set aside.
2. Heat the oil in a large pan and fry the chopped onion, tomatoes, pepper and garlic.
3. Add spices to taste.
4. Add plantains. Cover and simmer over low heat until plantains are tender.
5. Serve hot.

Source: Food.com

Tagine

Morocco

There's a restaurant called Latitude 31 in Marrakech, Morocco (186, Rue El Gza Arset lhiri Bab Doukkala). As one of our favourites, we even adopted the name for the *WhatsApp* group I have with my brother and sister-in-law since 2016. This secret hidden location in a courtyard, the food was incredible. Like many food outlets in the area, no alcohol is served here. Their Tagine was faultless.

Anyway, I digress.

Tagine is actually the clay or ceramic vessel in which many Moroccan dishes are traditionally cooked. Whilst many people also use normal pans or slow pressure cookers, a tagine looks like a pointy hat on a flat plate.

The stew, also referred to as *tagine*, often includes lamb, but the vegetarian version below is equally nice.

Prep time: 15 mins
Cook time: 40 mins
Serves: 4 - 6

Ingredients:
- ☐ 1/4 cup extra virgin olive oil
- ☐ 2 medium yellow onions, peeled and chopped
- ☐ 8–10 garlic cloves, peeled and chopped
- ☐ 2 large carrots, peeled and chopped
- ☐ 2 large potatoes, peeled and cubed
- ☐ 1 large sweet potato, peeled and cubed
- ☐ Salt to taste
- ☐ 1 tsp ground coriander
- ☐ 1 tsp ground cinnamon

- ☐ ½ tsp ground turmeric
- ☐ 2 cups canned whole peeled tomatoes
- ☐ ½ cup chopped dried apricot
- ☐ 1 quart low-sodium vegetable broth (or broth of your choice)
- ☐ 2 cups cooked chickpeas
- ☐ 1 lemon, juice of
- ☐ Handful fresh parsley leaves

Method:

1. In a large heavy pot, heat olive oil over medium heat. Add onions and increase heat to medium-high. Sauté for 5 mins.
2. Add garlic and all the chopped vegetables. Season with salt and spices.
3. Cook for 5 mins on medium-high heat, mixing regularly with a wooden spoon.
4. Add tomatoes, apricot and broth. Season again with just a dash of salt.
5. Keep the heat on medium-high, and cook for 10 mins. Then reduce heat, cover and simmer for another 20 to 25 mins or until vegetables are tender.
6. Stir in chickpeas and cook another 5 mins on low heat.
7. Stir in lemon juice and fresh parsley. Taste and adjust seasoning, adding more salt to your liking.
8. Transfer to serving bowls and top each with a generous drizzle of extra virgin olive oil. Serve hot with your favourite bread, couscous, or rice.

Source: Themediterraneandish.com

Taste of Europe

Scotch Egg

United Kingdom

Of course, I had to include something from the United Kingdom. After all, I've lived here through my teens to adulthood, experiencing all kinds of food, from my first authentic fish and chips to the British version of a curry.

One of the best 'first-times' of trying something new was when I tried a *Scotch egg* in a typical English pub. I don't think it was the best one I've had, but it certainly started my feelings of excitement every time I see one on a menu.

Despite its name suggesting that this food is from Scotland, the *Scotch egg* actually originated from Northern Africa. Shocking, I know.

Apparently, this famous egg, wrapped in sausage meat and fried in breadcrumbs, may have derived its name from it being 'scorched' rather than being Scotch.

Original recipes also involved fish, rather than meat. Interestingly, it also has an uncanny resemblance to an Indian dish called *nargis kofta* which is covered in minced meat, instead of sausage meat and served with a gravy.

> **Prep time:** 20 mins
> **Cooking time:** 20 mins
> **Serves:** 4

Ingredients:

- ☐ 5 large free range eggs
- ☐ 300g pork sausage meat
- ☐ 1 tsp black peppercorns, crushed
- ☐ 140g cooked ham, shredded
- ☐ 25g sage, apple and onion stuffing mix
- ☐ 1 tsp chopped sage
- ☐ 1 tsp chopped thyme
- ☐ 1 tsp chopped parsley
- ☐ 100g plain flour, seasoned, plus extra for dusting
- ☐ 100g dried breadcrumbs (preferably Paxo)
- ☐ Sunflower oil, for frying

Method:

1. Bring a pan of salted water to a rapid boil, then lower 4 of the eggs into the pan and simmer for 7 mins 30 secs exactly.
2. Scoop out the eggs and place in a bowl of iced water, cracking the shells a little (this makes them easier to peel later).
   Leave them to cool completely, then peel and set aside.
3. Put the sausage meat, pepper, ham, stuffing and herbs in a small bowl, mix to combine, then divide into 4 equal balls.
4. Squash one of the balls between a piece of cling film until it's as flat as possible.
5. One at a time, lightly flour each cooked egg, then use the cling film to help roll the sausage meat mixture around the egg to completely encase it. Repeat with the other boiled eggs.
6. Crack the last egg and beat, then add to a flat dish.
7. Put the flour and breadcrumbs on 2 separate plates.

8. Roll the encased eggs in the flour, then the beaten egg and, finally, the breadcrumbs.
9. Heat 5cm of the oil in a wide saucepan or wok until it reaches 160°C on a cooking thermometer or until a few breadcrumbs turn golden after 10 secs in the oil.
10. Depending on the size of your pan, lower as many eggs as you can into the oil and cook for 8-10 mins until golden and crispy.
11. Drain on kitchen paper, leave to cool a little, then serve halved.

Source: bbcgoodfood.com

Pastéis de Nata

Portugal

Whenever I'm in Portugal (or *Nando's*), I know I'll be returning a little heavier.

The food, wine and these little *pastéis de nata (pastel de nata* in singular) – caramelised custard tarts – in Lisbon were mostly to blame for my rounder face in the holiday photos.

The best ones come from Belém, just outside Lisbon, where they apparently originate from.

Prep time: 30 mins
Cook time: 30 mins
Serves: 6 (assuming you stop at 2 tarts each)

Ingredients:
- ☐ 1 sheet pre-rolled puff pastry
- ☐ ⅓ cup all-purpose flour
- ☐ ¼ tsp salt
- ☐ 1½ cups of whole milk
- ☐ 1⅓ cups white sugar
- ☐ ⅓ cup water
- ☐ 6 large egg yolks
- ☐ 1 tsp vanilla extract
- ☐ 1 cinnamon stick
- ☐ 1 lemon, peel only, cut into strips
- ☐ Optional ground cinnamon for dusting on top

Method:

Preheat your oven to 550°F / 290°C, and lightly grease a 12-cup muffin tin.

Custard mixture:

1. Whisk the milk, flour, and salt together very thoroughly and cook over medium heat, whisking constantly, for about 5 mins or until well combined.
2. Take off the heat and let cool for 10 mins.
3. Once cooled, whisk in the egg yolks.

Sugar syrup:

1. Add sugar, water, vanilla extract, lemon zest, and cinnamon stick to a saucepan and cook until a cooking thermometer reads a temperature of 220°F / 100°C. Don't stir.
2. Remove the cinnamon stick from the custard mixture and add the sugar syrup to it and mix it until everything is well-combined.
3. Strain the mixture into a measuring jug.

Combine:

1. Cut the puff pastry sheet into two pieces and place them on top of each other.
2. Tightly roll the sheets into a log, from the short side.
3. Next, cut the log into 12 evenly sized pieces.
4. Place one piece in each of the 12 wells of the muffin tin.
5. Dipping your thumb in cold water first, press your thumb down into the centre of the dough piece and press outwards to form a cup with the pastry.
6. The pastry cup should have its top edge just above the top of the well of the muffin tin.

7. Fill each pastry cup ¾ of the way to the top with the custard and sugar syrup mix.
8. Put the tray in the oven and bake until the custard starts to caramelise, blister and the pastry goes golden brown (around 10-12 mins).
9. Serve warm, with powdered sugar and ground cinnamon (both optional).

Source: Spanishsabores.com

Guinness Cake

Ireland

This may be stating the obvious, but Guinness has been around for centuries and originates from Dublin, Ireland. It's now brewed in over 50 countries around the world.

I travelled to Dublin over St Patrick's weekend, a celebration held around 17th March for the foremost patron saint of Ireland, Saint Patrick. My visit to the Guinness Storehouse there, was educational to say the least.

Apart from the two free pints of Guinness that were included in the price of the entry ticket, I watched a céilí dance performance, and walked through misty rooms that reminded me of my school Chemistry classes.

Guinness' flavour comes from malted barley and roasted unmalted barley. Whether you're a fan of its taste or not, you can barely taste Guinness in this chocolatey cake. I can confirm that it is delicious.

> **Prep time:** 10 mins
> **Cook time:** 45 – 60 mins
> **Serves:** 8 - 10
>
> **Ingredients:**
> - ☐ 250 ml Guinness
> - ☐ 250g unsalted butter
> - ☐ 75g cocoa powder
> - ☐ 400g caster sugar
> - ☐ 150 ml sour cream
> - ☐ 2 large eggs
> - ☐ 1 tbsp vanilla extract
> - ☐ 275g plain flour
> - ☐ 2½ tsp bicarbonate of soda

Method:

1. Preheat the oven to 180°C / 350°F, and butter and line a 23cm / 9-inch spring-form tin.

2. Pour the Guinness into a large wide saucepan, add the butter – in spoons or slices – and heat until the butter's melted, at which time you should whisk in the cocoa and sugar. Beat the sour cream with the eggs and vanilla and then pour into the brown, buttery, beery pan and finally whisk in the flour and bicarb.

3. Pour the cake batter into the greased and lined tin and bake for 45 mins to an hour. Leave to cool completely in the tin on a cooling rack, as it is quite a damp cake.

4. When the cake's cold, sit it on a flat platter or cake stand. The cake can be served with or without icing.

Source: Nigella.com

Did you know...

- Guinness is a type of beer known as 'porter' or 'stout porter' or just 'stout'. It was very popular with porters in London in the 18th century, hence the name.
- It's not black… if you hold up your pint glass up to the light, you'll notice it's very dark red in colour. Surprise!
- It is rich in iron and antioxidants.

Part Three: Explore Life

Life
/lʌɪf/ noun

The condition that distinguishes animals and plants from inorganic matter,
including the capacity for growth, reproduction, functional activity, and
continual change preceding death.

Explore Life

Travelling and exploring the world, with all its cultures, people, languages, cuisines and landscapes, is essentially a channel for us to benefit from more knowledge, awareness and joy.

I have experienced phases of travelling 'too much' (yes, it is possible) as well as not travelling enough.

In either situation, I would feel like my life was slightly off-balance, which made me slightly anxious. So, I realised the importance of examining how travelling fits into our lives, as a component or ingredient of a balanced life.

This section summarises specific concepts, life hacks and frameworks that could help you ensure that you feel like you're in control of your life, before you incorporate 'travelling' into it.

The three main concepts include:

Concept ONE: Detachment
Concept TWO: Taking Action
Concept THREE: Sources of Happiness

These concepts should help you make the appropriate arrangements to be able to do more things that you love; be it travel, work, eat, exercise, or spending more time with certain people.

Concept ONE: Detachment

Over the last few years, I have learned that nothing is permanent.

Relationships, money, health and physical appearance are all things that many of us work hard to achieve and sometimes take pride in.

That's all fine, but if any of those are suddenly taken away from us, how would we react?

Would we just crumble and then acknowledge the loss with a view to taking the next steps to move on with life? I know it's easier said than done, but we must try, instead of accepting defeat.

Having a level of detachment from the people and things in our lives and being self-contained are ways of preparing for the best and worst times.

I'm not suggesting that we stop having emotions, but the less you are dependent on others, the less likely you are to have a long-term life crisis.

Taoism

Taoism, or Daoism, is a philosophical tradition of Chinese origin which encourages people to embrace life with grace.

It suggests that the past and future are not part of who you are. It is only the present moment in time that matters and should determine your mind set, mood, happiness, and so on.

Loss

Losing sucks.

Whether it's a game, a challenge, a race, losing possessions like your valuables or luggage while travelling, or, worst of all, losing someone we love.

Sometimes – if not every time – when we lose something, we miss it. That misplaced bracelet you threw on the side of the bed, which you now wish you hadn't thrown, or the friend you didn't make enough effort to meet or contact, who is no longer there.

We forget to appreciate what we have, until we lose it; or if you're lucky, almost lose it. Whether it's health, wealth or loved ones.

Over the last few years, quite a few people I know have lost things that are important to them in their lives. I've seen the strength required to deal with death of loved ones, job losses, broken relationships, and so on. Yet people move on, mainly because they have to.

Loss is a big deal, especially as it leaves behind a void that has the potential to consume our entire brain. We will all face loss in one form or another, so it's important to keep some methods of crisis-management and a level of detachment, at hand.

Concept TWO: Taking Action

Make Your Bed: Small things that can change your life by William H. McRaven is a book about things that helped him overcome challenges in his career and his life in the Navy.

Doing one task first thing in the morning, such as making your bed perfectly, can kick-start your day on a good note. It makes you feel like you've already achieved something.

Conclusions:

- ☐ Start each day with a task completed.
- ☐ Find a companion to help you through life.
- ☐ Respect everyone.
- ☐ Remember that life isn't always fair and you'll often fail or lose.
- ☐ Take some risks.
- ☐ Step up when times are tough and never give up.
- ☐ Face up to the bullies.
- ☐ Be around people who make you happy.

Concept THREE: Sources of Happiness

Buddhism

According to Buddhism, a relatively neutral religion, there are three key sources of happiness:

1. **Consciousness:** living in the moment. Focus on now, rather than the past or future.

2. **Good company:** make good friends and find people who help you grow.

3. **Truth:** be honest about what matters to you.

Four Pillars of Happiness:

During a TED talk, author, Emily Esfahani Smith, cited another example of how to live a meaningful life by illustrating four pillars:

Pillar ONE: Belonging

This comes from relationships, where you feel valued for who you are.

Pillar TWO: Purpose

This involves using your strengths to serve others and see an impact through your contribution.

Pillar THREE: Transcendence

This is linked to experiences beyond the norm, such as spiritual awakenings, feelings of trance, or just realisations.

Pillar FOUR: Story-telling

How you define and tell the story of your life, choosing to keep the parts you want to keep and deleting the ones you don't (applies to the past and future).

These four pillars, if well-constructed on an ongoing basis, could be a good way to look at your life and work towards feeling joy on a more regular basis.

Article: Balance
Excerpt from srtravels.co.uk

Balance

[ˈbal(ə)ns] Noun
*An even distribution of weight enabling someone or
something to remain upright and steady.*

Just like the Disney character *Bambi*, we all learn how to
become more stable over time, sometimes with the help of a
guardian or friend.

If you're reading this book, you're probably not young
enough to be told what to do by your guardians, parents,
teachers etc. on a daily basis. To be fair, even my three-year-
old nephew won't always do what we ask of him.

The responsibility to find the right balance in our lives lies in
our own hands, which can be daunting, but also liberating.

How do we make better decisions about different aspects of
our lives to make sure we remain upright and steady, at least
most of the time?

Here are a few examples that some of you may be able to
relate to.

Eating well

The world is increasingly health-conscious. It can be
tiresome to look through every single nutrition label to see if
what I'm about to eat is good or bad for me.

As life is too short to be reading small print every day, I've
decided I could do other things to have a more balanced
diet, such as eating more home-cooked meals, maintaining a
respectable portion-size and drinking more water.

Work vs. Life

Many of us have a job; mainly for practical reasons such as paying for our passions such as travelling. Our careers often involve achieving personal and professional goals. These could include responsibilities, positions, salaries, professional networks or qualifications.

Working crazy hours towards career progression can feel like it's for a good cause, but there may come a point when the feeling of satisfaction plateaus. Suddenly, the realisation hits after a number of years have passed, that you've missed out on other parts of your life, like family or health.

You vs. Others

In terms of prioritising others versus yourself, it's important to address your own needs. Before we can be balanced and strong enough to give attention to others, we need to give ourselves the attention, care and love required to stay upright and steady.

After all, there is no practical reason to give to charity while you starve yourself.

Now vs. Future

While it's important to have a bird's-eye view of your future plans and a general idea of where you see yourself in life, try not to obsess about this.

Enjoy the good moments, deal with one day or a week at a time, trying to appreciate at least one good thing every day that you're looking forward to, or have achieved: all of these little things can help us enjoy life a bit more.

The Life Balance Wheel

The objective to obtain balance is a key reason for protecting ourselves.

We can create invisible cushions to avoid unnecessary pain and drama. If we fall, we can bounce back without causing permanent damage.

The 'Life Balance Wheel' is a practical visual tool that can help evaluate how balanced your life is at that specific moment. This can also highlight the areas that may need some extra attention.

Remember, it's important not to place yourself under unnecessary pressure to be good in everything at one time. By doing this, you risk facing 'burn-out'.

At the back of this book, you will find a template of a 'Life Balance Wheel'; you can build this yourself.

Further reading:

- *Fear: Essential Wisdom for Getting Through the Storm* – by Thich Nhat Hanh
- *Mindfulness: A practical guide to finding peace in a frantic world* – by Mark Williams
- *The Power of Now: A Guide to Spiritual Enlightenment* – by Eckhart Tolle

Article: Selfish
Excerpt from srtravels.co.uk

Selfish
/ˈsɛlfɪʃ/ adjective
A person lacking consideration for other people; concerned chiefly with one's own personal profit or pleasure.

Depending on the circumstances, I believe that being selfish can have its own benefits.

When we travel by air, the safety demonstrations include specific instructions on:

- How to buckle your seat belt.
- How to inflate your life jacket in case of emergencies.
- How to put on your oxygen mask.

Although most of us will hopefully never have to use a mask or life jacket, there are important life lessons in this particular metaphorical example and others, of how being selfish can sometimes be a good thing. Here are three:

Lesson ONE: Survival
Lesson TWO: Mental balance
Lesson THREE: Runaway Money

Lesson ONE: Survival

Before helping others, always put your own oxygen mask on first. This includes helping children and those who are less able.

Basically, if you can't breathe and take care of yourself, you probably won't do a great job helping someone else. That to me, is good-selfish.

Lesson TWO: Mental balance

Another example of good-selfish is taking care of our mental balance. There is no point in spending hours and days helping others, listening to their troubles, when it's dragging you down and making you feel low or miserable.

When we notice this happening, we should take a break. A break could mean being present physically for someone going through a crisis, but actively not engaging with their emotions.

Detachment can help us during fragile times. This may sound less empathetic, but when it comes to taking care of ourselves, others can only help so much.

For instance, I don't think I could have a permanent job at a mental asylum or special needs centre, as I don't think I would be able to handle my emotions on a regular basis. I have tremendous respect for those who work in such situations, and admire their mental strength.

Lesson THREE: Runaway Money

This is another example of how a degree of independence, whether you're male or female, old or young, is essential for many reasons, including self-respect and more balanced relationships with others.

I once read something about 'runaway money'; in essence, this means extra cash for yourself only, in case you ever want to run away or take a break from a job, relationship, country or situation.

Needing to take a break or getting away does not make us bad people. We can still share everything else with others.

Runaway money can give you the reassurance that if everything blows up, as unlikely as that may be, and you're on your own, you'll be okay. It minimises the need to be needy or dependent, and removes an element of insecurity.

It could also minimise the chances of others regarding you as a burden. They may even get some reassurance that you're with them because you want to be, not because you need to be. Well, at least from a financial point of view.

In conclusion, *good-selfish* is when the situation requires you to look at the bigger picture and do what you need to do.

This will ensure that you're able to be yourself 100 percent and, therefore, potentially benefitting those around you, including yourself.

Article: Time, Intent, Action
Excerpt from srtravels.co.uk

Over the years, I have observed the behaviour of others and myself and I noticed a few things that I think are worth taking the time to write about.

Making time for priorities

When you do not or cannot give something (or someone) your time, it is worth asking yourself if you have genuinely prioritised them in your life.

Sometimes, you may be spread too thin and it's impossible to give our time to others or our long 'to-do' lists. However, a routine check is always helpful to ensure that we don't end up neglecting vital people or duties, leading to negative consequences.

At times, we also forget to prioritise ourselves. I know at least three people who have had gym memberships for several months, but haven't been more than a few times. Apart from being a total waste of money, it shows how they are not giving time to their health as a priority.

Intention

If you *really* want to make an effort with a project, a person, a relationship or even a challenge, like travelling the world, there is no question that you'll do everything you can to make it happen.

If you become complacent, and your intent is weak, it probably won't happen; or may not happen soon enough If it does happen, it may not be as great as it could have been if you'd given it 100 percent dedication.

Act

Very rarely do things just happen magically or by themselves. So, do something about your intentions and dreams.

- ☐ Write down what needs to be done.
- ☐ Note down a deadline.
- ☐ Do something towards it, even if just one task.

In short, I hope I've been able to go beyond stating the obvious: when we want something enough, we should do anything except nothing, and do it sooner rather than later.

Article: Bye Bye
Excerpt from srtravels.co.uk

My little nephew once walked into a room full of (too many) children, screamed in disgust and said: *'Bye, Bye!'* before trying to escape.

This illustrates how a child can clearly communicate what he wants to walk or run away from.

Saying no, or walking away from things and people you're not sure you like, or that are making you uncomfortable, probably doesn't happen as often as it should.

Knowing when to stop, or when to stop someone or when to say no can help minimise complexity and negativity in our lives. Without realising, being 'too nice' can prolong dysfunctional projects or relationships.

Anything that we think affects us negatively, should be eventually minimised or removed from our lives.

From personal experience, I feel I've had situations where I built up anger towards people, scenarios and, even, myself, which could have been avoided if I'd walked away earlier, or just said no. Here are FOUR lessons on what to say 'Bye, Bye' to:

Lesson ONE: Bad Haircuts
Lesson TWO: Onions
Lesson THREE: Linear Paths
Lesson FOUR: Busy Bees

The Hungry Traveller

Lesson ONE: Avoid Bad Haircuts

This is a reference to the speech from the chick-flick movie, *Legally Blonde 2.*

Towards the end of the movie, Elle, played by Reese Witherspoon, gives a speech about the reason behind a bad haircut she once had. She explains that it wasn't the stylist's fault, but her own.

She could have involved herself earlier in the process, trusted herself in what she wanted and spoken up to stop the stylist from ruining her hair further.

This applies to manicures, pedicures, massages – any situation where we pay for something but don't receive good service.

I sometimes still say "it's fine", when a masseuse asks if the pressure is OK. However, in reality, I am actually in borderline pain.

The reason for this behaviour is that I was avoiding an uncomfortable conversation and situation – but at my own expense.

The lesson here is to say, *'Bye, Bye!'* to 'bad haircuts' by speaking up at the right moment.

Lesson TWO: No more Onions

When there is an imbalance in the effort put into a relationship, or if someone has crossed the line more than once, you should not refrain from telling them how their behaviour made you feel.

Try not to wait for years before taking action. We should consider doing this without haste, in the right moment, calmly and politely.

Here are 10 signs that you may be ready to let go of someone or something – like a situation that makes you cry:

10 types of 'Onions':

1. Feeling undervalued
2. Settling for less
3. Exhaustion
4. Loss of joy
5. Scared of change (and loss)
6. Regularly sad
7. Feeling trapped
8. Living in the past
9. Not putting yourself first
10. Low expectations

If we can see and feel that a relationship has lost its base, is broken, hurtful and doesn't involve mutual trust and respect, maybe it's time to say, 'Bye, Bye!' in the interest of everyone involved.

Lesson THREE: Think Beyond Linear Paths

As a child, linear paths have been assigned to most of us with good intentions. A standard life path involves:

A child is born, goes to school, college, graduates, gets a job, gets married, has children, retires, has grandchildren and, eventually, dies.

What if I don't want to go to university and want to start working straight after college?

What if I don't want to be a doctor, engineer, banker or lawyer?

What if I want to travel and it delays me finding a job and having an income straight after graduating?

These are all things that we should consider, alongside our circumstances and practicalities.

If you do end up sacrificing your passions for a job that pays the bills, it's important to try and see how you can squeeze your passions into your life.

It's easy to say, "quit your job and travel the world", or "become a painter". However, there is a fine line between being brave and being stupid. We need to make informed decisions about risks at certain points in our lives.

Lesson FOUR: Busy Bees

Sometimes, we can be guilty of over-committing ourselves and our time to others, to the point that we are spread too thin. This can take a toll on our health.

Over the last few years, I've gotten better at declining meetings (or 'tentatively accepting' which basically means, I won't show up). All these have been done with good reason.

Being busy gives people a 'buzz' and it's certainly beneficial to converse with people, share thoughts and ideas. However, being too busy and not having enough time to rest physically and mentally, can cause stress, anxiety, depression, headaches, insomnia... and, in extreme cases, heart attacks!

So, say *'Bye Bye!'* to the unnecessary meetings when you can.

Some things to potentially say *'Bye Bye!'* to:

- ☐ Bad service
- ☐ Unnecessary meetings
- ☐ Physical challenges that you don't enjoy
- ☐ Pretentious places
- ☐ People who make you feel worse
- ☐ Large group chats
- ☐ Overcrowded places
- ☐ Socialising out of politeness
- ☐ Unfulfilling jobs

Everyone has priorities in life which are unique to them. What you add to or remove from your life is often in your hands.

The Hungry Traveller

Article: Friends of Seasons, Reasons and Life
Excerpt from srtravels.co.uk

When I was much younger, my mother explained to me that in their school, they used to pick a *sakhi* (सखि), which means 'a friend for life' in the Hindi language.

In this age of cynicism, we may think it's idealistic to have a *sakhi* or two.

Some people are lucky to still have friends from school as they progress through adulthood. While others have friends from university, places they've worked, travelling acquaintances, wedding, a retirement home, a supermarket and so on.

It doesn't matter when, where or how you befriend someone, sometimes it can take a long time to learn about the kind of friendship you share with them.

The Test

The true test of friendship is often: Time.

I don't necessarily believe in categorising friendships. However, in hindsight, we could gain a general idea of the purpose certain people have served in our life.

Retrospectively, we need to think about whether certain people have already served their purpose in our life (or vice versa) (**Friend of Reason**); Were they there during a phase of our life? (**Friend of Season**); Have they been with us through various phases and they don't seem to be going anywhere, anytime soon (**Friend for Life**).

Change

Whether it's a reason or season, it's important that we accept that sometimes relationships, including friendships, have expiry dates and are impermanent.

Some friendships gradually fizzle out, while others can end in ways that are more dramatic and painful for one person or everyone involved.

There could be situations where the foundations of a friendship have been broken, either intentionally or unintentionally. Despite individual or mutual attempts to fix them, things can never go back to being how they used to be. That's when you know the friendship has come to an end.

What I've learnt from experiences like these is that we need to stay clear of two things:

- × Blaming the other(s)
- × Blaming yourself

Neither helps the situation.

Instead, we can make peace with the way things are. We can compartmentalise the people who are no longer our friends in a *Reason* or *Season* box, and move on, taking away any lessons learnt.

As mentioned in the **Four Pillars of Happiness**, we have control over the 'story' we tell ourselves and others, about our lives and the people who were in it.

If we choose to, we can focus on the pleasant memories of the good times, accepting that as part of our story. With this in mind, we can carry on with life.

We can then move forward, prioritise and invest in the people and relationships that are still in, or are about to come into, our lives.

We can make 'change' work for us.

Friendship Recipe

Preparation time: a lifetime
Serves: minimum of 2 persons
Instructions: try not to forget the ingredients.

Ingredients:
- ☐ A jar of kindness
- ☐ A spoonful of listening
- ☐ A can of honesty
- ☐ A tube of trust
- ☐ A carton of patience
- ☐ 1kg of forgiveness
- ☐ A box of encouragement
- ☐ A pot of respect
- ☐ A bag of loyalty
- ☐ A bottle of fun (and sometimes...rum.)

Source: Teachingideas.co.uk

Apart from certain family members, in moments of joy and crisis, good friends can also form a strong support group.

Tara Brach, a respected author and meditation teacher mentioned in one of her podcasts (*tarabrach.com*, 2019):

"*Sangha* is the word for good company, which could help you grow and be happier."

Article: Lessons from a Baby
Excerpt from srtravels.co.uk

In 2016, I was introduced to a new member of the family: my nephew.

Even when he couldn't talk, he certainly communicated his point in some form. Before I knew it, he'd reminded me about a few things that could make life a bit easier:

1. **Be Real**

   My nephew doesn't 'fake smile' or cry for no good reason. When you try to make him laugh, if he doesn't find it funny, he won't laugh. When he does smile and laugh, we know he really means it.

   Equally when he cries, we know something is wrong.

2. **Stop eating when you're full**

   I wouldn't suggest spitting out the food in your mouth when you're full, or throwing it on the floor like he does, especially in public.

   Nonetheless, when your stomach is full, there's no benefit from overeating.

3. **Hugs**

   I personally love a good hug. I can swear by the effect it has on your mood, depending on who or what you're hugging.

   My nephew enjoys a cuddle from his approved list of people who can come near him.

"We need four hugs a day for survival. We need eight hugs a day for maintenance. We need twelve hugs a day for growth."

- mindbodygreen.com

4. One step at a time

I watched my nephew crawl-climb up stairs for the first time. Measuring each step with his little legs, he gradually increased the number of steps that he covered in every future attempt he made.

There was no rush, no panicking, just slow, individual baby steps that helped him reach his ultimate goal: his Grandma, who gave him plenty of hugs.

5. Travel

Having been to eight countries by the time he was two years old, my nephew is already a bit of an explorer.

It's a shame he won't remember any of his trips as a baby, but hopefully he'll carry on travelling when he's older. By exploring different places, people, food and culture and, perhaps, reliving the trips that he can't remember.

6. Learn from your mistakes

If he bumps his head on the same bar stool more than twice, we would be surprised.

He carefully avoids the obstacle afterwards, and carries on with a new route. It's an example of perseverance and learning from mistakes.

7. Laugh more

When little children laugh, you'd need to be dead inside if you didn't crack half a smile.

It's very infectious. Sometimes their laughter is for no reason whatsoever.

A bird, a bulb, someone's hair... anything can set my nephew into fits of laughter, with an inevitable domino effect on the rest of us around him.

Laughter, like hugs, is another free source of endorphins (happy hormones), so we need to let ourselves laugh at every opportunity.

I'm sure there are other things to learn from babies and young children; eating and sleeping on time, making sure you keep some time aside to play, asking questions, crying for help... the list keeps growing.

The bottom line is, we were all young(er) once. Just because we're all much older and independent, doesn't mean the rules have changed.

Just have a conversation with the next baby or young child you meet and you'll get the reminder you may need.

Your turn...

If you've made it this far through the book, this is the perfect time to start jotting down some ideas for your future.

Here are some templates to help you visualise or plan what you want to see, eat or do more of.

Happy travelling, eating and living!

Where Have You Been?

Mark all the places you have been with a dot and those you would like to visit with a cross.

After you visit a place marked with a cross, draw a circle around the cross and colour it in. This turns your "intention" (cross) into another achievement(dot).

Key:

⊗ I want to go here
● I have been here

Your Travel Progress Bar:

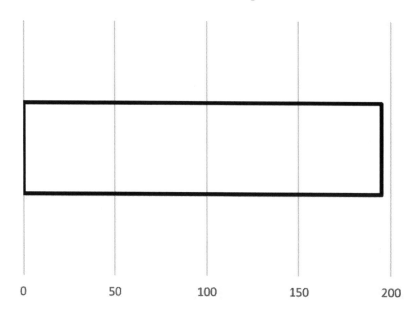

Key:

 Number of countries I have visited.

Your Life Balance Wheel:

This practical visual tool could help you evaluate how balanced your life is right now. This can also highlight the areas that may need extra attention.

Instructions:

1. Draw a circle and divide it into 8 – 10 sections, depending on your main priorities in life.
2. Based on the level of satisfaction you feel in each category, rate yourself between 0 – 10 (0 = least satisfied, 10 = completely satisfied). Shade the area up to the approximate rating number.
3. When you mark yourself out of 10 in each of these areas, you can quickly identify the areas that require your extra focus in the near future i.e. anything that rates 0 – 6 on the scale.

Feel free to cross out some of these sections and replace it with your own. For example, based on you own priorities, you may wish to include or delete travel.

Once you complete the wheel, you'll be able to visualise which areas of your life you need to focus on. I would suggest reviewing the wheel every three months to a year. However, this is your wheel; it's your choice to revisit whenever you feel like it.

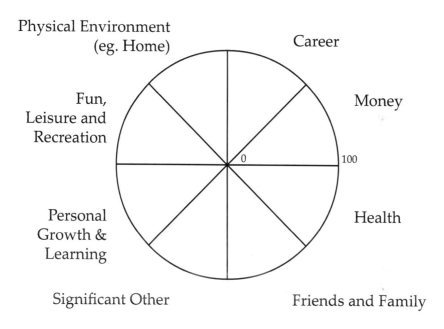

Key:

Level of satisfaction

Your Favourite Recipes:

Name	Country	Page no.
_____	_____	_____
_____	_____	_____
_____	_____	_____
_____	_____	_____
_____	_____	_____

A to Z

Adventure
/ əd'vɛntʃə/ noun
An unusual and exciting or daring experience.

Backpacking
/'bakpaking/ verb
A form of low-cost, independent travel.

Carbon Footprint
/ˌkaːbən 'fʊtprɪnt/ noun
The amount of carbon dioxide released into the atmosphere as a result of the activities of a particular individual, organization, or community.

Destination
/ˌdɛstɪ'neɪʃ(ə)n/ noun
The place to which someone or something is going or being sent.

Ecotherapy
/'iːkəʊθɛrəpi/ noun
Treatment intended to improve your mental and physical wellbeing by performing outdoor activities in nature.

Foodie
/'fuːdi/ noun
A person with a particular interest in food; a gourmet.

Gringo
/'grɪŋgəʊ/
In Spanish-speaking countries and contexts, chiefly in South America, this is a person, especially an American, who is not Hispanic or Latino.

Hodophile
[Greek] / adj.
Lover of roads.

Inertia
ɪˈnəːʃə / noun
A tendency to do nothing or to remain unchanged.

Journey
/ˈdʒəːni/ noun
An act of travelling from one place to another.

Kingdom
/ˈkɪŋdəm/ noun
A country, state, or territory ruled by a king or queen.

Life
/ˈlʌɪf/ noun
The condition that distinguishes animals and plants from inorganic matter, including the capacity for growth, reproduction, functional activity, and continual change preceding death.

Migration
/mʌɪˈgreɪʃ(ə)n/ noun
Seasonal movement of animals from one region to another.

Nomad
/ˈnəʊmad/ noun
A person who travels from place to place and has no permanent home.

Opportunity cost
[Economics] / noun
The loss of other alternatives when one alternative is chosen.

Panorama
/panəˈrɑːmə/ noun
An unbroken view of an entire region surrounding an observer.

Que sera sera
/ˈeɪ sərɑː sərɑː/
Future events are out of our control.

Rendevous
/ˈrɒndɪvuː,ˈrɒndeɪvuː/ noun
A meeting at an agreed time and place.

Selfie
/ˈsɛlfi/ noun
A photograph that one has taken of oneself, typically taken with a smartphone or webcam and shared via social media.

Transcendence
/trɑːnˈsɛnd(ə)ns/ noun
Existence or experience beyond normal or physical level.

UN SDGs
[Acronym]
UN Sustainable Development Goals (SDGs) are a collection of 17 global goals designed to be a "blueprint to achieve a better and more sustainable future for all". Introduced in 2015 by the United Nations General Assembly, it is predicted that the SDGs will be achieved by the year 2030.

Visa
/ˈviːzə/ noun
An endorsement on a passport indicating that the holder is allowed to enter, leave, or stay for a specified period of time in a country.

Wanderlust

/ˈwɒndəlʌst/ noun
Originally a German word meaning a strong desire to travel.

Xerophilous
/ˈzɪˈrɒfɪləs / adj.
Plants or animals adapted for growing or living in
dry surroundings.

YOLO
[Acronym]
You only live once. It is a call to live life to its fullest extent, even
embracing behaviour which carries inherent risk.

Zoogeny
/ˈzəʊˈɒdʒɪnɪ / noun
The doctrine of the formation and evolution of animals or
living things.

Sources: Collins Dictionary; United Nations; Google; 2019

Printed in Great Britain
by Amazon

58395678R00099